Cake and Hamster

Annie Burchell

Copyright © 2022 Annie Burchell

All rights reserved. No part of this publication may be reproduced, stored in any retrieval system, or transmitted, in any form or by any means, electronic, mechanical, photocopying, recording or otherwise, without the prior written permission of the author.

This book is a work of fiction. Names, characters, businesses, organisations, places, and events other than those clearly in the public domain, are either the product of the author's imagination or are used fictitiously. Any resemblance to actual persons, living or dead, events or locales is entirely coincidental.

Cover design and illustrations by Vince Reid

With love to Bea, who only quite likes bananas.

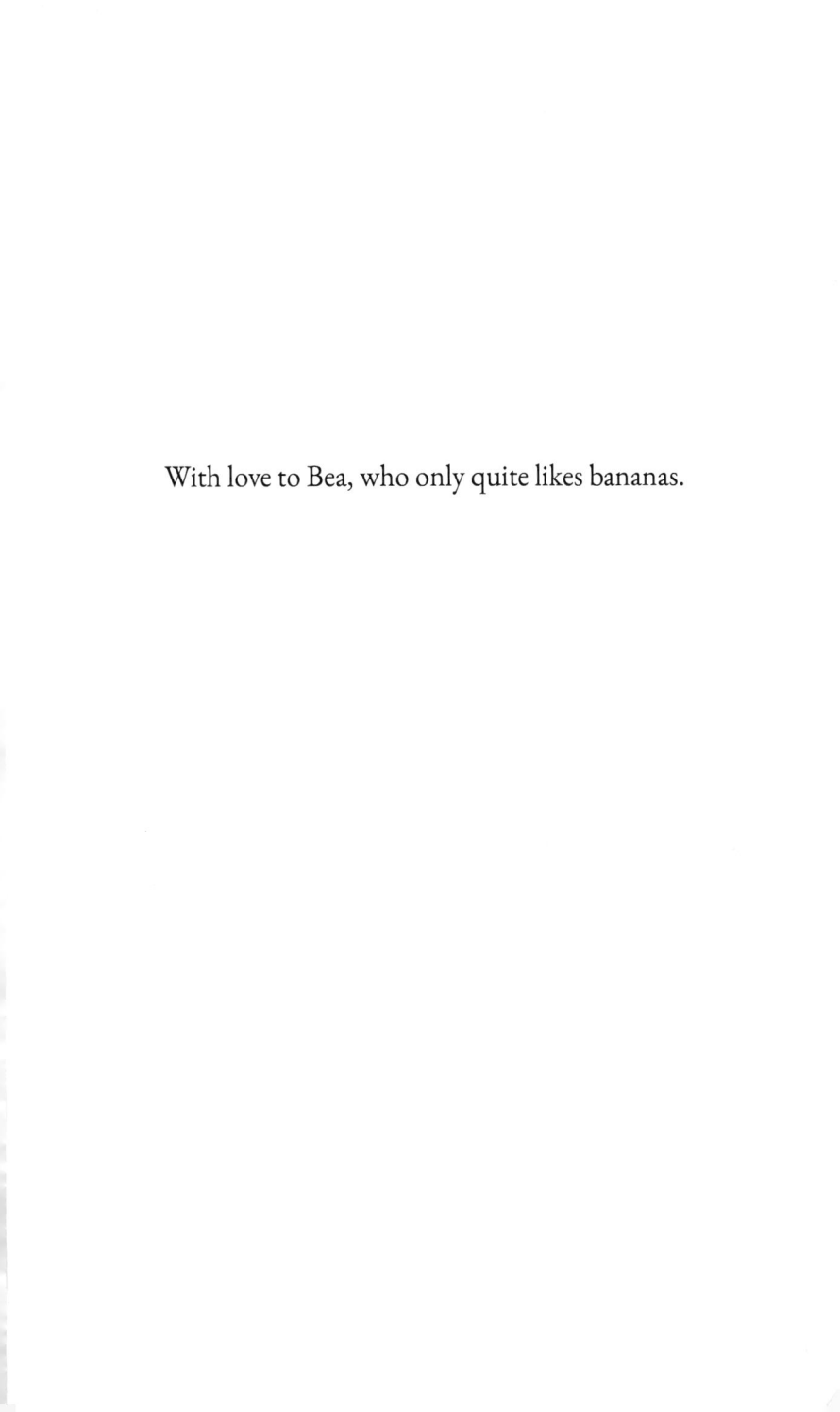

Chapter 1

Looking back, I can see how stupid I was now.

It all started about two weeks ago in school assembly. I was just sitting there wondering who invented the flip-flop, when I was jolted out of my daydream by a strange noise.

'What was that?' said Amrita, looking over at the far side of the hall.

It didn't take me long to realise what the noise was. It was the faint gasps of astonishment that were echoing around us as Mrs Collins, the head teacher, made her way to the stage. At first, I couldn't work out quite what was going on, but as soon as she came into view, I knew immediately what had happened.

'Mrs Collins has been to the hairdresser's again,' I said, my eyes wide with excitement.

'Uh-oh,' said Oscar. 'What's it going to look like this time?'

I'm always eager to see what Mrs Collins has had done to her hair for one VERY good reason. I have what hairdressers call unmanageable hair and what my little brother, Max, calls mad scarecrow hair. So, for me, Mrs Collins' never-ending quest for the perfect hairstyle is actually quite inspiring.

This time, her 'new look' was truly spectacular. From the back, it looked like she'd been involved in a collision with a candyfloss machine. From the front, it was more like a butternut squash. I began to wonder whether I was looking at the future of hair. Perhaps one day Mrs Collins would be regarded as one of the great hairstyle innovators of our time?

I decided right there and then that I would ask Mum if I could get a fluffy butternut squash next time I went to the hairdresser's. She's always telling me I need to act more grown up because I'm going to be twelve in a few months.

And surely nothing says responsible grown-up girl more than having vegetable-shaped hair!

When Mrs Collins reached the stage, the muttering died down, and she gazed warmly around the room.

'Good morning, children,' she trilled enthusiastically.

'Good morning, Mrs Collins,' we droned back at her.

'To start this morning's assembly, would you all please join me in singing hymn No. 7.'

Since the start of the school year, we've had to sit in girl/boy order in assembly. Unfortunately, I'd drawn the short straw that morning and was sitting next to Alex Bentley. I wouldn't want you to get the wrong idea about Alex – he's not a nightmare or anything. In fact, he's actually OK for a boy. It's just that he tends to get a bit overexcited when he's singing. He sings REALLY loudly. But that's not all. He FLAPS his elbows up and down while he's doing it. There's no nice way of saying this, but he looks A LOT like a giant baby bird – wearing a school uniform – attempting to fly for the first time.

I have no idea why he does this. Perhaps he thinks his elbows control the volume of his voice via a series of wires. But anyway, it's not a particularly relaxing experience sitting next to someone who's singing at the top of their voice while trying to take off!

After a couple of very long hymns – made to feel even longer by Alex Bentley's big baby bird impression (sorry, Alex!) – Mrs Collins stepped forward and made some announcements. It was mostly the usual stuff – no running in the corridors, table manners at lunchtime and band practice, etc.

'And finally,' said Mrs Collins cheerfully, 'I have some very exciting news.'

Now, I like Mrs Collins, but her idea of what counts as exciting can be a bit UNUSUAL. Previous so called 'exciting' up-and-coming events have included a lecture on dental hygiene from a local dentist, a new carpet in the library and a talk on CLOUDS (yes, you heard me, CLOUDS). But today's announcement was genuinely surprising.

'We've decided to hold our very own baking competition here at Melton Primary School!' she said proudly. 'But make sure you get your name down early. There are only a limited number of places available, and the competition starts next week.'

Even I had to admit that was a bit exciting. And I wasn't the only one. As a wave of chatter swept around the hall, Mrs Collins paused for a moment and beamed contentedly. She was listening to one of her favourite sounds in the world – the sound of enthusiasm.

At the time, I thought the baking competition just seemed like a bit of harmless fun, but if I'd known how the next two weeks were going to play out, I may not have been quite so relaxed about it. You see, due to my own stupidity, I got involved in something that turned into a bit of a nightmare. But to help you understand how it happened, I should probably tell you a bit more about myself.

For history homework that weekend, I'd had to write a fact file on King Henry VIII, which wasn't difficult because, let's face it, he had a pretty full life. If I had to write a fact file on myself, it would probably go something like this.

FACT FILE

- Name: Cordelia – although most people call me Cordie, unless they're a teacher or my parents and I've really messed up. Then they call me Cordelia Roberts in a very cross voice.

- Age: 11½

- Home life: I live with my mum and dad, my annoying younger brother, Max, and a hamster with a surname.

- Star sign: I want to say badger (but I may have got that wrong).

- School: I'm in Year 6 at Melton Primary School. I quite enjoy school because, like my mum, I'm a bit of a nerd. And I have not one but TWO best friends, my fellow nerds, Amrita and Oscar.

- Likes: Chocolate (I was once asked to leave a well-known chocolate shop because they said my dribbling was upsetting the other customers); prime numbers (see, I warned you I was a nerd); and daydreaming.

- Dislikes: PE (and anything that looks, sounds or smells remotely like PE).

- Additional information: For the purposes of this story, the most important thing you need to know about me is that I have a tendency to blurt things out without thinking first. Mum sometimes calls me 'The Blurter', which I actually quite like because it makes me sound like a superhero. But instead of using my superhero powers to save an entire city from a hooded baddie who lives in some sort of underground cavey thing, I just tend to get myself into trouble.

What I'm going to tell you now is about a particular time when my mouth really ran wild and got me into very hot water. It's a long story, so I'd better start at the beginning. Well. Where else would I start? But before I do, I should probably say something like:

SOME NAMES HAVE BEEN CHANGED TO PROTECT THE INNOCENT.

I noticed this at the beginning of a film once and thought it was quite cool.

Anyway, it all began at Friday morning break, not long after Mrs Collins had made her announcement in assembly...

Chapter 2

There was quite a buzz going around the school that morning. Everyone was talking about the baking competition. And I would have been too, if it hadn't been for one small detail.

I CAN'T BAKE.

Most of my previous attempts at baking had been a complete disaster. But then, not being very good at baking is a bit of a tradition in my family.

My aunt Miriam once had to call the fire brigade out after the red velvet cupcakes she was making actually CAUGHT

ON FIRE! How can you make something as cute and harmless as a cupcake go on fire, I hear you ask? It's hard to say since, thankfully, I wasn't there. But I do know that the entire block of flats where she lives had to be evacuated, and she hasn't been able to bake since. Not because she was traumatised by the incident, but because her neighbours all signed a petition asking her to stop!

And then there's Gran. How can I describe Gran's baking without being rude?

I could do that thing grown-ups do when they want to tell you the truth, but they can't because they've got to be polite. If I was doing that, I'd probably say her baking is ECCENTRIC. And if I was doing the whole just-being-me thing, I'd probably say it was a bit BONKERS. But then that would be unfair because there's one part of baking that Gran's really good at and that's pastry making. But more of that later...

When I reached the playground at morning break, I looked around for Oscar and Amrita. We met on our very first day of school and became best friends soon after when we realised we had one of the strongest bonds it's humanly possible to have. We're all really bad at PE! In fact, the only thing we ever argue about is who's the worst. But as far as

I'm concerned, there's only one clear winner – me! I just know I'm the best at being the worst at PE. I'm so bad I could probably win some sort of medal for it!

After scanning the playground for a few seconds, I spotted Oscar and Amrita waiting for me in our usual spot. Or should I say our NEW usual spot? We had to move from our previous spot because Amrita thought the tree that hangs over that part of the playground was a 'spider risk'.

'If we stand under it for too long, spiders might fall on us,' she said. 'And even if actual spiders don't fall on us, we'll probably get covered in "spider-related stuff".'

So we decided to move.

It was probably for the best, anyway. It was hard to relax when we were standing under the tree. Every few minutes Amrita would suddenly lurch forward and waft her arms around like a startled orangutan, shrieking, 'Get it off me! Is it on me? Get it off me!' Yes, I think it's fair to say that Amrita isn't the 'outdoorsy' type.

Not being a nature lover hasn't stopped her from being good at just about everything else, though. Oh, except getting out of wigwams (see below). If I had to write a fact file on Amrita, it would go something like this.

FACT FILE
- Name: Amrita

- Skills and talents: BRILLIANT at all subjects. AMAZING at singing. Great problem solver. Excellent in a crisis, unless it involves any of the things listed below under 'Dislikes'.

- Likes: Being indoors where it's nice and safe and clean and there are no insects.

- Dislikes: Insects; spiders; bacteria; heights; the outdoors; PE; and wigwams.

- Additional information: Amrita once got stuck in a wigwam at her cousin's birthday party (no, I have no idea why anyone would have a wigwam at their birthday party either). While she thrashed about frantically trying to escape, the wigwam collapsed on top of her. She's still convinced that the whole thing was some sort of plot by the insects and always refers to it as 'The Great Wigwam Insect Conspiracy.'

As I made my way across the playground, I noticed Oscar was waving frantically at me.

'Hurry up, Cordie,' he shouted, gesturing for me to move more quickly. 'This is important!'

By the time I reached Oscar and Amrita, having skidded half the way there on a trail of discarded yogurt (sorry, shoes!), Oscar was practically bursting with excitement.

'So, are you entering then?' he asked, looking like he was about to explode.

'Do you need the toilet?' I said. I knew he didn't, but I wanted to draw attention to the weird jiggly dance he was doing.

'Please stop talking about needing the toilet,' Amrita pleaded, screwing up her face. 'It reminds me of the girls' toilets and the flying spiders.'

Oscar and I looked at one another for a moment, and I knew we were thinking exactly the same thing – 'Oh no, not the flying spiders!'

Let me explain. In Year 2, Henry Walker once told Amrita that there were flying spiders in the girls' toilets that would probably land in her hair and build an entire city by home time. Not surprisingly, none of this happened because:

1. there's no such thing as flying spiders;

2. even if there was, I doubt if they would be organised enough to construct a city the size of Tokyo within a few short hours, and;

3. even if I turn out to be wrong about 1. and 2., I'm sure there'd be something squirty you could buy from the chemist to get rid of them.

'Are you entering the competition?' Oscar screeched, his face beginning to turn red with frustration.

'I don't know,' I said. 'I'm guessing you are?'

I really didn't need to ask that. It was fairly clear from the fact that Oscar was now hopping from foot to foot like a rabbit at a sponsored dance-athon that he was probably already planning a five-tier hedgehog-themed wedding cake.

'Of course I am!' he bellowed. 'And if you want to be in it, you'd better get your name down today. It starts next week and there aren't that many places available.'

As ridiculous as the idea of ME in a baking competition sounded, I had to admit that it would be fun baking with Oscar because he's so enthusiastic about everything. And, more importantly, we'd also have access to A LOT of cake. But I couldn't, could I?

'I need to think about it a bit first,' I said. 'I'm not really a baker. I've only ever baked a couple of times and they were both disasters.'

'Oh, come on, Cordie,' he pleaded. 'It'll be a laugh AND we'll probably get to eat lots of cake!'

For someone so gangly and lean, Oscar has a truly enormous appetite. The trouble is, he's not very careful about how he gets the food into his mouth, so you can usually guess what he had as a snack just by looking at his face and clothes. I like to think of it as a fun game!

If I had to write a fact file about Oscar, it would probably go something like this.

FACT FILE

- Name: Oscar

- Skills and talents: SUPER CREATIVE (he's brilliant at English and art). He's also enthusiastic, optimistic and brilliantly goofy.

- Likes: Writing, doodling, chatting and eating (sometimes all at the same time).

- Dislikes: Sports, bushcraft, CAMELS.

- Additional information: His endless enthusiasm means he tends to act on impulse, which sometimes leads to disastrous consequences. And it's because of this that his catchphrase is 'Uh-oh!' Once had an encounter at a zoo with a camel that he still won't talk about. Oscar is sometimes referred to as 'Hula Boy' (but more about that later...).

'I assume you're not entering the competition, Amrita?' I said.

'Correct,' she answered without hesitation. 'Sharp knives and "burnie" things. It all sounds a bit dangerous to me.'

'It takes place indoors,' I said, 'so it'll be insect-free.'

'But what if it gets too hot in the kitchen and somebody opens a window?' she said, her eyes widening. 'The insects might notice the yummy baking smells and all come rushing in at once like some sort of massive insect tsunami! I'm sorry, Cordie – that's not a risk I'm willing to take.'

Chapter 3

It was at this point that Cleo Hawkins appeared with her two loyal sidekicks. What can I tell you about Cleo Hawkins? Well, although most of the teachers seem to like her, she's not always that popular with the rest of us. And she's never happy unless she's got someone in trouble – usually me.

Cleo's fact file would be something like this.

FACT FILE

- Name: Cleo Hawkins.

- Bad points: Quite showy-offy; often walks around

as if she owns the place; wears a bow in her hair that's so big it threatens to block out the sun and bring about the end of civilisation.

- Good points: Zero.

'You're not thinking of entering the baking competition, are you, Cordie?' she asked, flashing her best fake smile at me.

'I am,' said Oscar, leaning in and beaming enthusiastically.

True to form, Cleo ignored Oscar and kept her eyes trained on me.

'What about you, Cordie? Are you going to enter?'

'I don't know,' I said, trying to sound casual. 'I might.'

'Really?' she gasped, doing a very bad impression of someone who's shocked.

'Why do you want to know?' I said. I instantly regretted this because I could guess what was coming next.

'Well, it's just that I remember your biscuits from the bake sale. I nearly broke a tooth on them.'

To be fair, she was right. They were truly awful. I tried one and ended up with a funny taste in my mouth for the rest of the day. It reminded me of that smell you get when it rains for the first time in ages. I'm pretty sure I didn't put any wet lawn in them. At least it definitely wasn't in the recipe. Although I do have a tendency to lose concentration, so I guess anything's possible.

'But then I suppose not everyone can be a natural baker,' Cleo purred, stroking her glossy hair. 'My family says my Victoria sponge cake is to die for.'

'Well, we'll just have to keep our fingers crossed that nobody dies from eating it,' I answered.

It was one-all, I thought to myself. And I have to admit, I was enjoying the look of irritation on her face. Then, feeling a sudden rush of confidence at having levelled the score, I blurted something out without thinking.

'Do you know what? I think I will enter.'

'Good for you,' said Cleo mockingly. 'I'll make sure the local fire brigade are on standby.'

For some reason, this comment really pushed me over the edge. I hadn't been so annoyed since my little brother Max superglued my bedroom door shut, and started screaming through the keyhole that there was an alien in there.

'Fancy making the competition a bit more interesting?' I asked, allowing my irritation to get the better of me.

'Sure,' said Cleo. 'What did you have in mind?'

There was only one thing it could be. There was one thing that Cleo was absolutely terrible at... singing. Her singing voice is incredibly high pitched – in a way that can actually hurt your ears. And Cleo is VERY aware of this and massively embarrassed by it.

'How about the loser has to sing a solo in assembly in front of the entire school?' I suggested.

Cleo's eyes widened in horror, but she didn't waiver for a second.

'OK,' she snapped back at me, determined to save face in front of her friends.

Aha! I'd trapped her! Not only would this be her worst nightmare, but I also knew that Mrs Collins, the head teacher, would jump at the chance of a pupil singing a solo in assembly. She's always in favour of children 'being brave' and she loves to see us getting up and 'having a go'.

I was ridiculously happy... for about two seconds.

It was then that I realised – I hadn't actually trapped Cleo after all. I'd trapped myself because I CAN'T SING EITHER! But worse than that, I ALSO CAN'T BAKE! So it was more likely that I would lose the competition, and then have to get up and perform the stupid song MYSELF!

But it was too late to backtrack. With a flick of her hair, Cleo was gone, flouncing off across the playground with her two flunkies trailing along behind her.

I turned around to find Oscar and Amrita staring at me in silent horror. But I already knew what they were thinking. My big flappy mouth had done its big flappy thing.

'Oh no!' I said, opening the same big flappy mouth to speak. 'What have I done?'

The Blurter had struck again!

The rest of the day was a bit of a blur. I tried to concentrate on what the teachers were saying but images kept flashing into my mind. They were mainly of me up on the stage singing VERY badly, while a smug-looking Cleo watched on enjoying my humiliation.

I was so distracted in Art that I got one of those plastic googly eyes stuck on my forehead. I tried everything to get it off but it just wouldn't budge. This was EXTREMELY annoying for several reasons:

1. I have no idea how it got there. We weren't even using them.

2. It's usually impossible to get them to stick to

ANYTHING and, even if you do manage to, they generally fall off three seconds later.

3. I had to spend the rest of the lesson looking like a Cyclops (OK, not a Cyclops because they only have one eye, but whatever you'd call something with three eyes).

Eventually, my teacher, Mr Pip, decided to tackle the googly eye problem. At first, I thought he'd taken pity on me, but it turned out he had his own reasons for wanting to deal with it.

'We've got to get rid of that eye,' he said. 'I don't like the way it keeps staring at me.'

So he borrowed something from Mr Bugler, the school caretaker, to try to remove it. The only problem was, he got it from the cupboard that's permanently locked and has a big sticker of a skull and crossbones on it with 'Danger!' and 'Keep Out!' written underneath.

Anyway, to be fair to Mr Pip, the stuff he used to get the googly eye off did work. But unfortunately, it left a BIG red target mark on my forehead for the rest of the day. On balance, I think I preferred the extra eye!

Chapter 4

I was even more relieved than usual when the week was finally over. I normally love Fridays but this one had been a disaster.

Let's recap.

At morning break, I had challenged the school's biggest princess-la-di-da-perfect-pants to go head-to-head with me in the school's baking competition. And I can't bake. I mean, I really can't bake. But that's not all. I had also suggested a forfeit, which meant that whoever lost had to sing a solo in front of the entire school. And I can't sing. I mean, I really can't sing.

Then at lunchtime, it turned out to be National Turnip Appreciation Day. Yes, I know what you're thinking – I couldn't believe it either – but it is an ACTUAL thing. And as one of the few vegetarians in the school, I was served what can only be described as something knobbly in a brown sauce. That's not what was written on the whiteboard menu, but that's definitely what it was. And there's worse...

For pudding, it was TURNIP AND SULTANA CAKE. That's right. You heard me. They put turnip in a cake! Now, they can mess with my savoury, but DO NOT TOUCH MY PUDDING! Pudding is sacred. I'd go as far as saying that custard is like a religion to me. Anyway, by the end of the lunch break, I'd eaten more turnip in one meal than I'd eaten for the entire time I'd been alive.

For the rest of the day, my stomach sounded like an angry donkey playing the banjo, if you can imagine that. In fact, try not to imagine that. Euugghhh!! And by the time I got the googly eye stuck on my forehead, my day of misery was complete.

As you can imagine, I wasn't in the best of moods when I met Mum at the school gates. And the look of horror on her face when I took my hood down and she saw the red mark on my forehead didn't improve things much, either.

'I got a googly eye stuck on my forehead,' I said calmly, before she could jump to the wrong conclusion. 'It's not as bad as it looks.'

'How does anyone get a googly eye stuck on their forehead?' she said, staring at me in disbelief.

'I wish I had a googly eye stuck on my forehead,' bellowed my little brother, which of course made everyone turn around and stare at the bizarre three-eyed creature.

I took a deep breath and tried not to let him get to me. Then I quickly put the hood of my coat back up and kept it there for the entire journey home. Of course, that didn't stop Max from quizzing me about my new third eye. And by the time we got home, I'd had enough.

'I think I'll get my homework done straight away,' I said, hoping this would put an end to all the googly eye chat.

The googly eye wasn't my only reason for offering to get on with my homework only two minutes after getting home from school ON A FRIDAY! You see, I've learnt over the years that actually doing the homework is less of a torture than spending the entire weekend being asked if I'm doing the homework, if I've already done it, or when

I'm intending to do it. So, getting it done early isn't as mad as it sounds after all!

And anyway, leaving homework until the last minute NEVER works out well for me. There was one time last term when I had a geography project that was due the next day, but I started it so late in the evening that I actually FELL ASLEEP while I was doing it! When I woke up, I had a papier mâché volcano stuck to the side of my head. Honestly, what is it with me and getting things stuck to my head! Mum and I eventually prised the thing off, but it was pretty flattened (the volcano, not my head). In desperation, I tried to convince the teacher that it had been hit by a meteorite. She didn't believe me though, and I can't really blame her. After all, the finished model looked more like a small mound with an imprint of an ear on it than a volcano.

To be fair, the homework I had to do over the weekend looked pretty cool. As well as the Henry VIII fact file, I also had to write an essay on what it would be like to be a domesticated animal. I decided to base the essay on my younger brother, Max. Living with him is like living with a small monkey, so I figured all I needed to do was watch him for half an hour and I should end up with lots of ideas!

The most important thing you need to know about Max is that he can be really, really annoying. A big part of this is because he's extremely LOUD. Our house isn't very big, and most evenings it's hard to find any private space to do my homework because of the constant noise he generates.

I don't really like doing my homework in my room because it's tricky finding my desk under all the mess. And if I lie on my bed to work, I know I'll just end up falling asleep – which is how the help-I've-got-a-volcano-stuck-to-my-head incident happened. So, I usually take my books and curl up in the armchair in the sitting room with them.

But it didn't take me long to realise that it's quite hard to write an essay about a small monkey when you're actually sharing a room with one. While I struggled to focus, Max was lying upside down on the sofa with his hamster, Colin (or Colin Hargreaves, to give him his full name.)

I once asked Max why Colin has a different surname to us, and he just looked at me like I was an idiot.

'We're not related,' he said.

And thinking about it, I guess I really should have worked that out for myself based on the overwhelming evidence that Colin is a HAMSTER!

I picked up my pen and tried to get started on the homework, but it wasn't easy because of all the noise that was coming from the TV.

Like most evenings, Max and Colin were watching their favourite programme, *Pigeon Attack!*

'Could you turn it down, please?' I asked hopefully, while also wondering how pigeons could be that noisy. 'I'm trying to do my homework.'

'I can't,' he bellowed. 'I can't find the remote control.'

'You're holding it!' I shouted.

'What?' he hollered back.

With his eyes firmly fixed on the screen, and not realising that he was already holding the remote control in his left hand, he felt around for it on the sofa with his right hand. He then picked up a VERY confused-looking Colin and pointed him at the screen.

'I don't think you'll have much luck changing the channel with Colin,' I said.

But he just ignored me, put Colin on his head, and carried on watching his demented pigeons. And there they sat like some sort of strange hamster and boy pyramid, enjoying their pigeon show. I decided to give up and head to my room for a bit of peace and quiet.

My little brother is fascinated by animals, and his hamster Colin goes everywhere with him. Well, at least he tries to take him everywhere. He's always attempting to smuggle Colin out of the house – sometimes with disastrous consequences for the rest of us.

A good example of this is the time we were thrown off a flight to Spain when Colin was found wriggling around in our hand luggage. He didn't even apologise (Max, not Colin). He said he didn't see why Colin couldn't have a 'hamster holiday', that rodents deserved mini-breaks too, and that everyone was just being 'anti-hamster'.

Mum and Dad were furious about what is now referred to as the 'Colin goes to Spain incident'. Mum was so angry that she actually told Max off in front of everyone at the airport.

'You're lucky we haven't sent you to Mr Burt's School for Naughty Boys,' she said as we made our way back to the car. Now, I can't be one hundred per cent certain, but I'm pretty sure this doesn't exist.

Dad was even more ridiculous. 'Somebody should invent a rodent detector to put in every airport around the world,' he said. I couldn't help thinking this was a slight overreaction and was also not very likely to happen.

Anyway, Mum and Dad have now taken matters into their own hands and have introduced what they call 'The Furry Friend Detection System'. This involves making my brother stand still in the hallway for a few minutes every time we're about to leave the house. They then watch him very carefully to check for 'suspicious wriggling' that may suggest he's got a hamster stuffed up his jumper.

But when it comes to Colin, nothing seems to put Max off. He is OBSESSED with him. In fact, he's now claiming he wants to be a HAMSTER TRAINER when he grows up. I keep telling him that's not 'a thing', but he just shakes his head and mutters about being ahead of his time.

'They laughed at Einstein, you know,' he always says.

Of course, he's right about that. They probably did laugh at Einstein, but I'll bet that had nothing to do with how crazy his theories sounded, and everything to do with the fact that he had funny-looking hair.

Back in my room, I cleared everything off the desk and settled down to do my homework. Of course, when I say 'cleared everything off the desk' what I really mean is I dumped it all on the floor. There was no space to put it anywhere else as my room is so full of STUFF. You see, I'm not very good at throwing things out. I like to think of my room as a historical record of my life. Mum, on the other hand, describes it as a SWAMP that should be fenced off to protect unsuspecting members of the public from falling into it and never being seen again. How very rude!

After spending time downstairs observing my brother, I felt ready to begin my essay on what it's like to be a domesticated animal. Working on the basis that Max is in fact a small monkey, I started by sketching out the options I had so far:

1. I'm a domesticated monkey who lives with two adults and an 11-year-old girl;

2. I'm a small hamster who lives with a domesticated monkey who, for some reason, seems to be obsessed with TV shows about pigeons;

3. I'm a domesticated monkey who thinks he's Albert Einstein and plans to open a hamster sanctuary at some point in the future.

In the end, I decided to write about a dog because my teacher, Mr Pip, is a big fan of dogs. And also, I didn't think he'd believe that I lived with a monkey – which is strange when you think about it because he knows I live with Max.

Still, at least this time I managed to finish the homework without getting anything stuck to the side of my head!

Chapter 5

I'd just finished my homework when I heard Mum calling up the stairs.

'Cordie, dinner's ready!'

After the lunch I'd had, I was hoping for something a bit less turnipy.

Mealtimes are usually fairly chaotic in our house. This is mainly because, at some point during the meal, there's a fair chance that Colin the hamster will burst out of my brother's pocket, leap onto the table and run across a bowl of mashed potato. I used mashed potato as an example because my family eats a LOT of mash. This wouldn't be a problem if we didn't also get bucketloads of the stuff at school. My little brother is delighted by this because mash is his second favourite thing after hamsters.

Don't get me wrong, Mum's cooking is actually really good; it's just that it can get a bit samey. But then she does have to make a veggie option just for me at every mealtime, which must be a real pain. She never complains about it though.

'It's nice to have a daughter who eats vegetables,' she said recently. 'Lucy's mum says she often catches Lucy feeding her leftover salad to the guinea pig. Apparently, she's been feeding him so much that he's put on weight and now the vet says he's got to go on a diet!'

I assumed Mum meant the guinea pig, not the vet.

Dad's cooking is a bit more adventurous, and it's also pretty good. But because he makes such a mess, Mum only lets him cook about once a week. Mum says she likes his cooking, but she doesn't like the fact that he leaves the kitchen looking like there's been an explosion in a custard factory! I must remember to ask Mum how she knows what an explosion in a custard factory looks like! It sounds AMAZING!

'How was your day then?' Dad asked as we gathered around the table.

'Well, school was boring,' said Max in his usual chatty way, 'but, since I got home, I've taught Colin a new trick, which is going to come in very handy when I enter him for the Hamster Olympics.'

'There's no such thing,' I muttered under my breath. I was careful to make sure he couldn't hear me say this. That way, I got the satisfaction of answering back without starting an argument.

'And lunch was cool,' Max continued.

'Oh good, what was it?' asked Dad.

'Sausage and mash.'

'How many sausages did you get?'

'Three!' Max bellowed triumphantly.

'How about you, Cordie? Was it *The Usual*?' Dad asked, grinning.

'No. It was worse than the usual,' I said. 'Let's just say it involved vast amounts of turnips.'

'It looked like the pond sludge we collected at forest school,' Max added helpfully.

'Yikes,' said Dad.

The Usual Dad referred to is the school's attempt at providing me with a balanced vegetarian diet. Unfortunately, it generally involves them giving me a WHEELBARROW full of roasted vegetables in a tomato sauce. It's basically the same meal every day, but they just give it a different name.

For example, Monday might be Vegetable Casserole; Tuesday could be Italian Style Vegetables; Wednesday would probably be something like Vegetable Hot Pot; and Thursday is usually Vegetable Curry. And if they can't even be bothered to pretend, they just call it 'Vegetable Medley'.

And then there's Fridays, when the vegetarian option is usually veggie burgers. I know this probably sounds like a big improvement, but it's really just leftover roasted vegetables squished together. AND they look nothing like burgers. They look more like FEET! In fact, come to think of it, they smell a bit like feet, too!

'What did the "Turnip Surprise" come with?' asked Dad.

'Insane amounts of mash,' I said with a grimace. 'What's on the menu tonight, Mum?'

Mum hesitated for a moment, clearly trying to find the right words.

'Erm, well, the good news is there are no turnips.'

'What about mash?'

'There may be some mash,' she whispered.

'How much mash?'

'Quite a lot of mash,' Mum replied, sheepishly.

'Whoah! It's a double mash day!' Max shouted, waving his arms in the air and then high-fiving Dad.

During dinner, Mum announced Grandma would be coming to stay with us for a few days. Apparently, she had been doing some home improvements in her house and, let's just say, it hadn't gone entirely to plan. Anyway, she now needed to get the builders in to deal with the DAMAGE, and she'd decided to move out while the work was being done.

This was GREAT news because I LOVE having Gran to stay. You see, she's a lot of fun, and most importantly she always carries a never-ending supply of sweets in her GIGANTIC handbag! I'm not kidding. Her handbag is HUGE and stuffed with all sorts of random things. I tried lifting it up once and almost sprained my wrist!

'Why is Grandma moving out of her house?' Max asked, while desperately trying to keep hold of Colin, who was now attempting to clamber up onto his head. 'Has it blown up then?'

'Not quite,' replied Mum patiently.

'Has it gone on fire?' he asked. Max was now under the table trying to reason with Colin as Dad glared at him disapprovingly.

'No, it hasn't "gone on fire",' said Mum.

'What happened then?' I asked.

'She was trying to hang a painting on the wall in the sitting room.'

'And?' I said gently, sensing that Mum was now looking embarrassed.

'And now the entire wall needs replacing.' Dad beamed and quietly chuckled to himself.

Then Dad suddenly stopped chuckling and leapt up out of his chair.

'Colin!' he yelled, as Max appeared from under the table, grabbing helplessly at Dad's sock and capturing Colin the hamster just before he disappeared up Dad's trouser leg.

'OK, that's it!' Dad said. 'He's going back in his cage.'

'But, Dad, he hates it in his cage,' Max protested.

'Well, he's going to have to get used to it when Grandma arrives,' said Mum. 'She's bringing Mr Wallace, the hungriest dog in the world, with her. And we don't want him mistaking Colin for a wriggly sausage.'

I'd forgotten about Gran's dog, Mr Wallace. Honestly, what is it with my family and naming pets? That was the only downside to Gran coming to stay with us. She was bringing Mr Wallace, the ravenously hungry dog. So, from the moment they arrived, we'd have to eat all our meals under siege conditions, nervously protecting our plates from a sudden lunge of a big, hairy dog mouth.

And then Mum reminded me of the other MAJOR downside to Gran's visit. How could I have forgotten? I would have to give up my room so Gran had somewhere to sleep. Don't get me wrong, I didn't mind giving up my bed for my dear old gran. The problem was that while she was staying with us, I'd have to sleep on an inflatable bed ON THE LANDING. I realise sleeping on the landing sounds crazy, but all I'll say for now is that there's a very good reason for it that involves a fridge and a rhinoceros.

And that's not all. Mr Wallace wasn't allowed in any of the bedrooms, so he had to sleep on the landing, too. This meant I'd be doomed to spend every night trying to stop a slobbery dog with a ridiculous name from eating my face!

After supper, I tried to take my mind off the sleeping arrangements by telling Mum about the baking competition at school. And I asked her whether she had time to help me prepare for the first round.

'It starts next week,' I said, 'and I haven't done any baking for ages.'

'It starts next week!' Mum said. 'Why can't they give us a bit more notice? They obviously think that parents have nothing better to do than rush around all weekend buying baking ingredients!'

'I'm sorry, Mum. I only found out about it today.'

'It's not your fault, Cordie. Look, I'd love to help you, but I'm so busy with work at the moment. Maybe you should ask Grandma to help? She taught me to bake when I was a little girl. Well, at least she tried, but I never really got the hang of it.'

The only problem with that idea was that Grandma's baking is a bit UNUSUAL. It's not that she's a bad cook; it's just that she can be a bit RANDOM when it comes to choosing ingredients.

For instance, if she really likes something, you'll get lots of it, and she'll put it in everything she makes. And because she's so good at making pastry, she likes to experiment with what she puts in pies. She once wrapped baked beans and Toblerone in pastry – although thankfully not together.

And, once, she even put yogurt in pastry. She called it her 'Yogurt Pie', and described it as being packed with 'yogurty goodness'.

So, as much as I enjoyed spending time with Grandma, I wasn't convinced that someone who wraps anything she can get her hands on in pastry and shoves it in the oven was the right person to help me prepare for the baking competition. On the other hand, she was very good at baking pastry, so I decided to keep an open mind.

Chapter 6

I tried to put the baking competition out of my head over the weekend, but when I woke up on Monday morning, the full horror of what I'd got myself into came rushing back to me. I just couldn't stop imagining myself up on stage singing really badly while Cleo and her friends sniggered at the back of the hall.

The walk into school didn't put me in a great mood, either. The light drizzle that spat away at us from the moment we left the house matted my hair to my face. It made me look like I was wearing some sort of bonnet they might have worn in olden times, only hairier.

But the worst thing about the journey was listening to my annoying little brother babbling on endlessly about the weather. You see, Max loves watching the weather forecast. The only problem is he doesn't always pay attention, so he often misunderstands what they've said. A good example of this would be last winter when he spent two whole days trying to convince us that LIZARDS were due to sweep across the country!

'I think you mean blizzards,' I told him.

'No, it was definitely lizards,' said Max. 'The BBC wouldn't make a mistake like that.'

When we finally reached the school gates, I could see Mrs Collins and her massive hairdo bobbing away in the distance.

For a head teacher, Mrs Collins isn't that scary at all. But then she doesn't need to be because we have Mrs Savage, the deputy head, for that. And even though Mrs Collins is supposed to be the one in charge, I think even she's a bit frightened of Mrs Savage. I know this because I once saw Mrs Savage tell Mrs Collins off for running in the corridor!

As we got closer to the main doors, I noticed Mrs Collins pointing out to a Year 3 boy that his tie was done up all wonky.

'Come on, Alexander,' she said encouragingly. 'You look so much smarter when your uniform is on properly.'

I'll never understand why we have to wear a tie at school. What's the purpose of it, anyway? It's not as though your shirt's at risk of falling off if you haven't got one on. Mum says it's supposed to be decorative, but our school tie most definitely isn't. It's green with purple stripes, and if you stare at it for too long, it makes you feel dizzy!

Despite my weird hair, my brother's bizarre weather chat, and wearing a tie that causes dizziness, I quickly cheered up when I remembered we had computing after registration. It's easily my favourite lesson because I love anything to do with computers, and it's not like any other lesson. And I have a theory about why this is that I'd like to share. It's taken me a while, but I've finally worked it out.

KIDS KNOW MORE ABOUT COMPUTERS THAN TEACHERS.

Well at least at our school they do. Whenever we ask Mr Pip a question about computers, he just mumbles something about 'Google' and wanders off.

I can't help thinking it would be more useful to the school if they got all the teachers together in a classroom once a week and let one of the Year 6 kids give THEM a lesson on computers. I'd be happy to help. I wouldn't even want to be paid. My only condition for doing it would be that I could set lots of homework, and any teacher who didn't deliver it on time would be given a detention. Just kidding, Mr Pip!

Chapter 7

As we headed out for morning break, I looked around the playground for any sign of Cleo Hawkins. The last thing I wanted was another confrontation with her, particularly after the hole I'd dug for myself over the baking competition. Fortunately, she's easy to spot. The bow in her hair is so BIG it's probably visible from space.

'Are you OK, Cordie?' asked Oscar. 'You look worried.'

'I'm fine,' I replied. 'I'm just trying to make sure we don't bump into Cleo Hawkins again. I don't want to get myself involved in any more stupid competitions. If I'm not careful, I'll end up challenging her to a race to see who can reach Mars first, or something.'

'Oh, don't do that,' said Oscar.

'Why, do you think I'd lose?'

'No, I'm sure you'd win. It's just that you'd never make it back in time for the bell.'

We met up with Amrita and the three of us started our daily wander around the playground, always making sure we knew exactly where Cleo was. Wandering about is one of the most popular activities during break time at Melton Primary, mainly because there's literally NOTHING else to do. In fact, I've become so good at it that if they introduced wandering as an event at the Olympic Games (which, let's face it, is a BIG 'if') I'm pretty confident I'd be in with a chance of winning a medal. I can just see it now...

'And the winner of the gold medal in the wandering event is Cordelia Roberts for the United Kingdom.'

After the rapturous applause had died down, and I'd failed to appear on the podium to collect my medal, the red-faced announcer would have to say, 'I'm so sorry, I'm afraid we can't find her. She must have wandered off!'

But just in case anyone gets bored of wandering (as if they would!), the school leaves out some equipment for us to use at break time. There are balls, hula hoops and skipping ropes, but you have to get out to the playground super quick to grab one before they're all gone. And, to be honest, it's hardly worth the effort, as most of it's quite bashed up.

By the time we arrived in the playground that day, there were only two items left. A football that was so battered it looked like a mutant hexagon, and a wonky hula hoop. Naturally, the hula hoop was completely off limits because of Oscar's infamous hula-hoop incident in Year 5.

Allow me to explain – and I know this is going to sound a bit odd – but Oscar once managed to get stuck in a HULA HOOP for an ENTIRE DAY. How, I hear you ask, do you get stuck in something that's mainly a HOLE? Well, he somehow twisted the hula hoop into a strange figure-of-eight shape while he was standing inside it before realising he couldn't get out.

Now, of course, the obvious solution to this was to just cut him out. But Mr Bugler, the caretaker, couldn't find his shears, which meant Oscar had to spend the rest of the day trapped in a hula hoop. He even had to eat his lunch in it. He took it quite well though because Oscar's a pretty laid-back kid. Anyway, it wasn't all bad. The dinner ladies felt so sorry for him that they gave him an extra pudding.

And he was freed just before home time, so at least he didn't have to get onto the bus wearing it. And that is the story of how Oscar came to be known as HULA BOY!

Oscar reached into his pocket and took out one of the baking competition leaflets that had been left on our desks when we arrived at school that morning.

'So, according to this sheet,' he said, 'we're in the last of the three groups and we'll be baking on Thursday. Lucky we got our names down when we did, because by the end of Friday's lunch break, all the places for the competition had gone. If we'd waited until afternoon break, we'd have probably missed out.'

'Yeah,' I said. 'And then my challenge to Cleo couldn't have gone ahead.'

I paused for a while so I could take in what I'd just said.

'OH NO!' I planted my face in my palm in despair.

'What's wrong?' said a startled Amrita. 'Is it a flying spider? Are we under attack?'

'No. It's not insect-related. Can't you see what I've done?'

They both shook their heads.

'All I needed to do to avoid going head-to-head with Cleo was to delay signing up for the competition, and I'd have missed out on getting a place.'

'Oh yeah,' said Oscar, with a tone that suggested it was all so obvious now.

It turned out I wasn't just an A grade maths student. I was also an A grade IDIOT! I began to wonder whether there was any chance I could get some back-dated house points for being an A grade idiot. If I could, I'd probably go straight to the top of the house point leader board.

They might even erect some sort of gold plaque (or maybe even a statue) to honour my achievements. I was just imagining my plaque in the school entrance hall, when Amrita woke me from my daydream with some of her usual straight-talking logic.

'Look, if you hadn't entered the competition, it would have looked like you were too scared to go up against her. So you've definitely done the right thing.'

Amrita was right. I didn't want to give Cleo the satisfaction of thinking I was frightened of her.

'Plus,' said Oscar, 'most of Year 6 know about the challenge now because Cleo and her crew have been telling everybody.'

Oscar was right, too. I didn't want the whole of Year 6 to think I'd backed down.

'Perhaps Cleo didn't get her name down in time to get a place?' I said, hopefully.

'Sorry, Cordie,' said Oscar, studying the leaflet again. 'She did get a place and, unfortunately, she's in the same group as us. But look, there are still three days to go before we have to bake, so the sooner you decide what you're going to bake, the sooner you can start practising.'

He went back to studying the crumpled leaflet. By now, Oscar was staring at it like my grandma's dog glares at my dinner.

'Right, let's see,' he said, sounding like an admiral planning a battle. 'There are three rounds in the competition, and they are biscuits, pastry and the grand final: celebration cakes. So, what are you going to do, Cordie?'

'Well, I'm glad you asked,' I said, in a voice that sounded like one of those TV chefs who get way too excited about a mushroom. 'I plan to bake something edible that won't make people throw up, and that doesn't end up catching on fire.'

They both laughed.

'How about you?'

Quick as a flash, Oscar gabbled out his response. 'First round triple choc chip cookies. Second round mixed berry pie. And finally, if I'm lucky enough to get that far, I'll be making a giraffe cake.'

He announced the giraffe cake SO casually that you could have almost believed it was a common thing, as if practically everybody was eating at least one giraffe cake a week. And I was just about to ask him what on earth he was talking about when...

'RAISIN!' shrieked Blake Hartley as he galloped past us.

Blake Hartley is the most annoying boy in the entire school. He's not horrible; he's just annoying. And 'Pass the Raisin' is one of the many irritating games he has invented.

The rules of PASS THE RAISIN are pretty easy to follow:

1. grab a mouldy raisin you've found on the ground;

2. pop it into the hood, onto the shoulder, or down the coat of your carefully selected victim;

3. scream 'RAISIN!' and run off.

See, couldn't be easier!

As you can imagine, this happens quite often at morning break because the playground is pretty much a carpet of raisins, orange peel and flapjack.

The unfortunate victim must then find someone else to pass the raisin on to. And, believe me, this isn't an easy thing to do when the entire school has scattered, and everyone's screaming 'RAISIN!' at the top of their voices. Failure to pass the raisin on results in you having been 'Raised' for the rest of the day. I know. I don't get it either. But all I can say is that, for some reason, it's really, REALLY annoying when you've been raisined.

It was Amrita's turn to get raisined that morning, and she wasn't very happy about it. For several seconds she shrieked and danced around like a Dalek at a disco with a small piece of dried fruit in the hood of its coat.

Eventually, her movements became so jerky that the raisin leapt out of her hood and flew up into the air. Up, up, up it went. And from that moment on, everything seemed to be happening in slow motion. The whole playground went silent, and everyone stopped and watched as the raisin then started dropping down again. Down, down, down it came until it finally dropped RIGHT INTO BLAKE HARTLEY'S OPEN MOUTH!

The crowd stood in stunned silence. Blake Hartley was still staring up at the sky with a look of utter confusion on his face. The inventor of Pass the Raisin had been raisined! In fact, it was more than that. He had been what can only be described as MEGA-RAISINED! As the shocked crowd slowly dispersed, he was still standing there frozen to the spot in horror, wondering how he would ever live this down.

Chapter 8

The rest of the morning was a bit of an anticlimax after that. Lunch was even more disappointing than usual, and not just because of the food. You can usually rely on Blake Hartley to do something ridiculous during lunch to lighten the mood. Sometimes he'll mould mash onto his eyebrows to make what he calls 'mashbrows'. Or he might just try and see how many peas he can balance on his head. Whatever it is, I have to admit, he usually manages to make me laugh.

But on this day, he wasn't doing ANYTHING. He sat in silence throughout lunch, clearly still in shock from having been raisined. The vacant expression on his face suggested that nothing in the world made sense to him anymore. It was as if he had looked deep into his soul and seen a raisin!

After a lunch break spent 'wandering', we headed back in from the playground. I was sure that the school day had probably peaked with the MEGA-RAISIN incident and everything was about to go downhill. And when I suddenly remembered we had PE next, I knew things were about to go downhill FAST.

'Oh great, it's PE next!' I said, beaming my most inane-looking smile.

Oscar and Amrita gawped at me and then looked at each other nervously.

'Just kidding!' I said. 'I thought if I said it out loud, I might start to believe it.'

'Don't do that to us,' said Amrita. 'That was really scary.'

'Yeah,' said Oscar. 'I thought maybe the PE department had reprogrammed your mind.'

'And how would they do that, exactly?' I asked.

'I don't know the precise details,' he said, grinning widely. 'They'd probably use some sort of machine that looks like one of those really big fridges, only with a huge lever on the side that sets off a series of flashing lights when it's pulled.'

We all laughed. It was going to take more than an oversized fridge with disco lights on the front to make us enjoy PE.

The interesting thing is we all have different reasons for not liking PE. Oscar doesn't like it because he's tall and has gangly limbs, which makes him a bit uncoordinated. Amrita doesn't like it because she'd prefer to be reading a book. Oh, and of course because it usually takes place outdoors in what she likes to call 'Insect Town'.

And me? I just think it's all a bit silly. I don't know why. Perhaps it's the jumping around getting sweaty, or maybe it's the fact that the PE teachers always seem to sound angry about something. Mum says it's just their way of encouraging us, but what if, like me, you're beyond help and just want to get through it without embarrassing yourself? Again!

Don't get me wrong, I'm not against exercise. I like walking and cycling, and swimming's good fun, too. I just don't enjoy PE. And I find things like running bizarre. I can only think of three reasons why you'd ever choose to run.

1. You're trying to catch a train.

2. You're being chased by a dinosaur.

3. You're trying to catch a train while being chased by a dinosaur, which makes perfect sense because you'd be trying to get on the train to get away from the dinosaur!

But I suppose if I'm honest with myself, the main reason I don't like PE is because I'M NO GOOD AT IT!

I'm bad at just about every sport there is. You name it, I can't do it. And I'm especially awful at gymnastics. I'm about as flexible as a broomstick, so when I try anything in gymnastics, it's basically like watching a pencil being snapped in half. Anyway, if you ask me, bending is not a sport. It's just a thing you have to do from time to time when you've dropped something.

As we stood in the drizzling rain, waiting for netball to start, my mind began to wander. To try and snap myself out of it, I walked over to the pile of equipment to get a netball bib. I didn't care which position I got, so I just grabbed a random bib, but for some reason it wouldn't come free from the rest of the bibs.

At first, I thought it was just tangled, so I kept pulling harder and harder, until eventually I realised that there was somebody on the other end. It was Cleo Hawkins. The bib I had randomly picked up was the captain's bib, and, of course, Cleo couldn't let anyone else be in charge. And just like that, we were suddenly in a TUG OF WAR.

'Let go of it, Cordie,' she growled. 'I had it first.'

'No, you didn't,' I spluttered. 'And you're not having it.'

This was one sporting event I was determined to win, but I knew it wasn't going to be easy. Cleo is much bigger than me. In fact, she's much bigger than anyone in the school, including some of the teachers! A crowd had started to gather, and I was becoming more and more aware that Mrs Barnaby (or Mrs Barmy as some kids like to call her) was nearby organising the netballs. It was only a matter of time before she saw what was going on.

As we struggled and strained, tugging back and forth, I gathered up my strength and gave a massive heave. As I did, Cleo gave me a crafty little smile before suddenly, and quite deliberately, letting go and crashing backwards onto the ground.

'Arrrggghh!' she cried out in pain, as she writhed in agony, holding on to her left leg.

'What is going on over there, Cordelia?' Mrs Barnaby bellowed. 'I will not have any messing around in my lessons. Ten laps of the courts. Now!'

While Cleo fake-limped over to Mrs Barnaby to get some sympathy, I was left to run ten laps in front of all the girls in my year group. I huffed and puffed my way around like a goldfish that had made the disastrous decision to step outside for some fresh air. And as I did, I could see Cleo grinning triumphantly in the distance.

That's it, I thought. *I've got to beat her in that baking contest now. BUT HOW?*

Chapter 9

When we got home from school at the end of the day, Grandma had already arrived. I knew this as soon as we opened the front door because I could see her HUGE handbag slumped in the hall with all sorts of random stuff spilling out onto the floor. Another clue that she'd arrived was the sound of her dog, Mr Wallace, frantically whimpering and scratching at my brother's bedroom door. He'd obviously worked out where my brother's hamster lived and was keen to get to know him a bit better. Max dropped everything and ran screaming up the stairs.

'Noooo!' he almost yodelled as he charged up them, taking two steps at a time.

Max had clearly decided that Colin the hamster was under attack from the forces of evil, and if he didn't get up there immediately, it would be CHOMPY-CHOMPY time for Colin. Usually, I'd think this was just another example of his hamster-obsessed mind overreacting, but, in this case, he was probably right. After all, there aren't any world-famous dog and hamster duos, and that's probably because of the old chompy-chompy issue.

When Grandma heard the commotion out in the hallway, she popped her head around the kitchen door to say hello.

'Hello, Cordie,' she said, 'what's up with poor old Max?'

'Oh, I think he's just in a hurry to say hello to Mr Wallace, Gran,' I said, quietly chuckling to myself. 'You know how much he loves animals.'

It's great when Grandma comes to stay. She's always so happy to see us, and she makes a real effort to take an interest in what we're doing – even though she sometimes doesn't completely understand. She calls WhatsApp 'Who's that', but at least she tries.

The only thing about Gran's visit that I wasn't looking forward to was sleeping on the landing. Now, you're probably wondering why I couldn't just sleep downstairs on the sofa. Well, let me explain. We have a VERY old fridge that makes a HORRIBLE low grumbling noise like an ANGRY RHINOCEROS. And when I tried sleeping downstairs last time Gran stayed, I spent the entire night drifting in and out of sleep, expecting a rhino to charge the sofa at any minute. Because of this, the only sleeping space left for me in our small house is upstairs on a draughty, narrow landing.

'It'll be exciting,' said Mum, when she tried to sell me the idea. 'Like going on a camping adventure, you know, like Bear Grylls.'

'Errrm, I'm sorry, Mum,' I said, 'I'm going to have to stop you there. I don't EVER remember seeing a Bear Grylls show called *Escape from the Landing*, where he has to survive for several days sleeping on an inflatable bed just outside his own bedroom door.'

Mum just smiled and said nothing. I knew from past experience this was Mum code for 'Thank you for taking the time to give us your feedback but it's happening anyway.'

'Why can't Max sleep on the landing?' I pleaded, in a last desperate attempt to save myself by sacrificing my little brother. 'It must be his turn?'

'You know why,' said Mum dismissively. 'The last time Max slept on the landing, he got up in the night and set up an adventure playground for Colin on the stairs. When Gran tried to go downstairs the following morning, she fell over an inflatable triceratops and sprained her ankle.'

I couldn't really argue with that. So, while Gran was staying with us, it looked like I was going to be stuck on the landing with Mr Wallace: a big, hairy, slobbering dog who makes every room he's in feel a lot smaller.

And I know this is going to sound weird, but for some reason Mr Wallace smells a lot like HAM. Now, this would make perfect sense if he only ever ate ham. But not this dog – this dog eats EVERYTHING. He eats bananas with their skins on, and he even chomps his way through chair legs. Gran claims this is actually very healthy because chair legs are made of wood and it probably counts as a good source of dietary fibre. I would argue that it isn't quite so great if you happen to be sitting on the chair when the chomping takes place. And trust me, I speak from personal experience!

One time when Gran was staying with us, we came home to find that Mr Wallace had eaten an entire bag of FLOUR. When we opened the door, the hallway was covered in powdery white footprints, but there was no sign of Mr Wallace anywhere. It was quite an easy crime to solve, though. We just followed the footprints through to the kitchen, where we discovered a nervous Mr Wallace hiding under the table, and he was looking much whiter than usual.

As a result of this strange and varied diet, he does what I can only describe as nuclear farts. I'm not kidding. Every time he farts, it's like being surrounded by a cloud of eggy gas. And he never owns up! He just lies there like nothing's happened. You know, it wouldn't even surprise me if his farts were in some way responsible for the melting of the polar ice caps. While we're all doing what we can to slow down climate change by reducing greenhouse gas emissions, the biggest threat to the planet is probably my grandma's flatulent dog.

I was just imagining Mr Wallace floating on a melting ice sheet powered by his own farts – while angry penguins and polar bears held their noses in disgust and waved their little fists at him – when I heard something rustling at the other end of the hallway. Gran was searching through her handbag-the-size-of-a-planet. This could only mean one thing. It was present time!

My grandma is the most generous person you are ever likely to meet. And she LOVES to give presents. Of course, because Gran's a bit what my mum calls 'left field' (which I think is a polite way of saying a bit bonkers) the gifts do tend to be quite random.

Some of the gifts she's given me over the years have included a book on gardening, a mug with a drawing of an angry donkey on it, and a spanner. That last one was particularly odd because I wasn't really into DIY at the time, mainly because I was only FOUR. Oh, and Gran's presents are ALWAYS accompanied by a bonus gift of a banana. Not only that, but she insists on wrapping the banana and sticking a bow on it because she says she 'wouldn't want to spoil the surprise'.

This unusual bonus gift is based on Gran's firmly held belief that EVERYONE LIKES BANANAS.

'Who doesn't like bananas?' she always says. 'Even monkeys like bananas!'

Other people look for an expert's opinion, or even a royal seal of approval to decide whether or not something's any good, but my gran would rather make her decision based on what monkeys APPEAR to like. I say appear to like because there's no way of knowing what monkeys actually like – mainly because they can't speak.

And anyway, it's not like they get much choice, is it? I mean they eat bananas because they either find them on trees in the wild or are given them by zookeepers. I've never once seen a monkey in the supermarket pushing a trolley around while carefully checking a shopping list that just has the word BANANAS written on it over and over again.

On this occasion, my presents from Gran consisted of a monkey-approved banana (obviously) and a tiny porcelain bell. I'm not sure what the bell was for. Perhaps it was for me to ring when I wanted someone to bring me more bananas?

And I have no idea what my brother got – although it's a fair bet that one of them was a banana. By the time presents were handed out, Max had barricaded himself into his bedroom with Colin. And as he sat in there keeping Colin safe, Gran's 'stink' dog waited expectantly outside, hoping for a yummy hamster snack.

Chapter 10

Once I had unwrapped my presents and eaten the curvy yellow one, I sat out in the kitchen while Mum made Gran a nice cup of tea.

'So, tell me all the news,' said Gran. 'We've got a lot of catching up to do.'

It had only been two weeks since we'd last seen each other, so there wasn't really that much to tell.

'How's school?' she asked.

'Oh, actually, there is something quite exciting happening at school. We're holding a school baking competition and I've decided to enter.'

'Well, that really is exciting!' she said, beaming back at me. 'Of course you're bound to win. To be honest, it's a bit unfair on the other children. They don't really stand a chance against you. But well done to them for trying, though.'

And that's one of the other great things about Gran. She's ALWAYS supportive, even when it's quite clear I'm completely rubbish at something. Obviously, this comes in particularly handy on sports day.

'Thanks for saying that, Gran,' I said, 'but the truth is, everything I've ever baked has been a complete disaster. Even Mr Wallace would think twice about eating it.'

'Well, it's lucky I'm here then because baking is what I do. I'll have to let you in on some of my baking secrets.'

'Oh, thanks, Gran,' I said, 'that'd be great.'

She stood up suddenly, with a mad glint in her eye. I knew what was coming next.

'In fact, let's do some now! There's no time to waste.'

'Ooooh, I'm not sure now's a good time,' I said, looking across at Mum, whose eyes had gone so wide at the mention of this that she now looked a lot like an owl.

And I suppose I couldn't really blame her for being horrified.

'The thing is, Gran,' I said, 'the last time Mum let me and Max bake something on a school night, we ended up having to order take-away pizza for dinner because the kitchen was in such a mess.'

'Yeah, that's right,' said Dad, poking his head around the door grinning. 'The council declared it a public hazard and shut down the surrounding roads.'

'That's not true,' I said in our defence.

'No, it's not,' said Mum, turning her owl-like glare in Dad's direction. 'And the last time your dad cooked dinner, he left the kitchen in such a state that when I arrived home from work, I thought we'd been burgled!'

There wasn't much Dad could say to that, so, for once, he didn't say anything.

But despite hearing all this, Gran was still determined to do some baking.

'Don't worry about us making a mess before dinner, dear,' she said. 'I've brought some of my PASTRY PIES with me. We can have those.'

Gran's home-made pastry pies are a legend in our house. The reason they're called pastry pies is that by the time they come out of the oven, Gran isn't always sure what she put in them. It's not that she can't remember, it's just that she's so focused on getting the pastry right she doesn't really pay that much attention to the filling. In fact, about the only thing she is sure of is that the pies are made from pastry!

The major downside to the pastry pie is that you often don't find out what's inside until it's too late. This can be particularly tricky for me because Gran hasn't really understood the whole vegetarian thing yet. Comments like 'I'm pretty sure there isn't too much meat in them,' or 'You can have chicken though, can't you?' and my all-time favourite, 'One sausage isn't going to kill you!' aren't exactly reassuring.

So it looked like supper was going to be another game of 'guess the filling'. But I was so grateful that Gran wanted to help me with the baking practice, I decided to worry about what might be lurking inside the pastry pie later.

Mum could see that Gran wasn't about to back down, so she reluctantly agreed to let us bake. But as we cleared a space in the kitchen and started setting up, it didn't take me long to realise that things might not go quite to plan.

To start with, you won't be shocked to hear that Gran suggested we make some banana muffins. To be fair, she'd brought so many bananas with her, it was probably a good idea to use some of them up. I'm not joking either – the kitchen looked like some sort of banana warehouse.

Unfortunately, Gran put way too much banana in, and the cake mixture ended up looking more like a smoothie than something that was going to turn into a muffin. But when I told Gran I thought it looked a bit on the runny side, she just laughed, shook her head, and trotted out her usual catchphrase.

'You can't have too much banana,' she said chirpily. 'Everyone likes banana!'

But that wasn't our biggest problem. At the exact moment we were taking our muffins out of the oven, the door burst open and Max bolted into the kitchen, followed by a very excited Mr Wallace.

'Get him away from me!' Max screamed, running behind the table. 'He's trying to eat Colin!'

Of course, Gran couldn't imagine her beloved Mr Wallace ever doing anything naughty, so she just assumed they were playing.

'Hello, Max,' she said, chuckling away to herself. 'Are you having a game of tag with Mr Wallace?'

As the fruity aroma of the banana muffins hit his doggy nostrils, Mr Wallace paused for a moment. He clearly couldn't decide what he wanted to eat first: a hamster snack or something more banana-ry. And before we could stop him, he'd jumped up at the kitchen table and started licking the lovely warm muffins.

At precisely that second, Colin slid down my brother's jumper and appeared, startled, right on top of the tray of newly baked muffins.

'Colin, no!' shouted Max. 'Come back!'

But Colin was now extremely panicked, and he began to run around so frantically that one of his little feet sank into a soggy muffin. The result was a terrified hamster stumbling about wearing what looked like some kind of strange CAKE BOOT, while being chased by a deranged dog.

So all in all, my first attempt at home baking hadn't been a great success. And we couldn't eat any of the muffins because they were covered in a combination of hamster footprints and dog dribble. But looking on the bright side, at least I wouldn't have a hungry stink dog, a nervous cake-boot-wearing hamster, a panic-stricken schoolboy and a banana-obsessed grandmother to deal with during the competition. At least I didn't think I would. I decided to check the rules, though, just to be sure.

On a more positive note, dinner was a great success. Gran's pastry pies turned out to be vegetarian because they were filled entirely with peas. So they weren't really pastry pies after all; they were PEA PIES. And, believe it or not, they were surprisingly tasty!

Chapter 11

Later that evening, I spent my first night sleeping on an inflatable bed on the landing. I didn't want to make Gran feel guilty for having my room, so I tried to act as if I was completely OK with it. But I knew I was going to be in for a rough night. And I was right. Gran's fart-powered dog spent the entire night looming over me, sniffing at my head. Every time I dozed off, I'd wake up to find him snuffling and grunting away at me again. It was bizarre – I just couldn't work out why he was so obsessed with my head.

After a terrible night's sleep, I was the first person to wake up the following morning. When I opened my eyes, I found Mr Wallace was still standing over me with a confused look on his face.

After a bit of a battle with the wobbly air bed, I eventually managed to stand up. But once I was on my feet, I noticed there were strange flakes all over my pillow. I patted my hair, looking for some sort of explanation, and more and more of the flakes fell to the floor like giant beige-coloured dandruff.

By now, Mr Wallace was going berserk, running around snuffling the flakes up with his big sloppy pink tongue. Eugghh! And then, just when I thought I couldn't have been more disgusted... THUD! A party-sized sausage roll tumbled out of my hair and dropped down onto the floor.

Mr Wallace pounced on it. And, as he did, he knocked me against my brother's bedroom door with such force that the door burst open, and I was catapulted into his room. Inside, I found Max curled up on his bed laughing hysterically. It didn't take a world-renowned detective to work out what had happened. Max had thought it would be absolutely HILARIOUS to sneak out of his room in the night and hide a small sausage roll in my hair.

Naturally, this drove 'the dog who eats everything' insane. And it instantly explained why he had been snuffling and snorting at my head all night. To make matters worse, Mr Wallace is also UNBELIEVABLY dribbly. When I saw myself in the bathroom mirror, my hair looked like I'd spent the night being attacked by a giant sausagey slug – which, when you think about it – I kind of had.

After showering off the sausagey slug gloop and getting dressed, I rushed downstairs. Thanks to my brother's sausage-roll trickery I was now running late for school, but I was still going to find the time to tell my parents that my OWN brother had deliberately hidden a sausage roll in his VEGETARIAN sister's hair so that she'd get attacked by a stinky dog.

I couldn't wait to see what punishment they'd hand out to him for his outrageous prank. No pocket money for a week? No screen time? Perhaps even no Colin the Hamster? It was difficult to know what they'd opt for, but one thing was certain: it was going to be a BIGGIE!

How wrong I was! We never really got on to the topic of what punishment my brother should get for his despicable crime, because every time I started talking about it, they couldn't stop laughing. That's right! MY

PARENTS found this hysterically funny. And the harder I tried to explain how awful it was, the funnier they found it.

'I don't know why you find this so funny,' I said. 'I'm lucky to still be alive.'

That was the final straw for Mum. She was now laughing so much that she had to leave the room. But I could still hear her snorting out in the hallway. And I think Dad would have joined her if he hadn't been crumpled over on the kitchen table with his head in one hand while slapping the table with the other.

After several minutes, they managed to pull themselves together and do a very poor impression of parenting.

'That was a very unkind thing to do, Max,' said Dad through stifled laughter.

'Yes,' said Mum. 'Don't do it again.' But I could tell she was still laughing on the inside because she had to contort her face into all sorts of strange shapes to hold in the giggles.

'Really! How unprofessional!' I muttered angrily to myself as I slumped down at the kitchen table.

At least Gran was supportive. To make up for my ordeal, she cooked me some pancakes for breakfast. Banana. OBVIOUSLY!

Thanks to my BROTHER, we left the house later than usual that morning. I was so worried on the way into school that we were going to be late for the register that I was practically RUNNING! And there wasn't even a dinosaur chasing us or anything. I REALLY didn't want to have to explain to Mr Pip and the entire class why I was late! Can you imagine!

Mr Pip: 'Why are you late, Cordie?'
Me: 'Because I had to wash my hair this morning after I woke up covered in flaky pastry and gloop, sir.'
Mr Pip: 'And why was that?'
Me: 'Because I slept on a wobbly bed on a landing with a fart-propelled dog, sir.'

The laughter would have been deafening, and I'd already experienced enough humiliation for one morning. Thank you, MUM AND DAD!

So, I was MASSIVELY relieved when we made it in on time for the register, even though I was also very disturbed by the fact that I'd nearly, accidentally, done some running on the way.

In history, we had to hand in the fact files on King Henry VIII that we'd done for weekend homework. I gave mine a quick read-through. And, if I do say so myself, I was pretty pleased with what I'd done – especially the part where under 'Hobbies' I'd written 'getting married'.

And then, as Mr Pip walked around collecting up the homework, something VERY strange indeed happened. An event so baffling that Mr Pip looked utterly confused by it. BLAKE HARTLEY HAD DONE HIS HOMEWORK!

A flustered Mr Pip hurried back to his desk and announced that he was going to read it out loud to the class immediately. Now, looking back, it would probably have been a better idea for Mr Pip to read it quietly to himself first. But he was so excited he just launched straight into it, and it didn't take long before we realised that Blake hadn't actually written a fact file about Henry VIII after all. He'd written a fact file about the Loch Ness Monster!

Mr Pip just shook his head. Blake was lucky we weren't being taught by Mrs Savage, the deputy head. She's so strict she once kept an entire class in at break time because somebody snorted!

While Mr Pip patiently explained to Blake the importance of reading instructions, my mind began to wander. I stared out of the window, and watched the school caretaker, Mr Bugler, as he did his strange caretaker stuff. He's been at the school for as long as anyone can remember, and yet nobody really knows that much about him.

I wondered what it would look like if someone had to write a fact file about Mr Bugler. It would probably go something like this.

FACT FILE

- First name: Mr

- Second name: Bugler (pronounced Bew-Gler. As in a musician who plays a bugle, which is a weird trumpety-looking thing.)

- Occupation: School Caretaker (involves taking care of the school. Clue's in the name).

- Likes: Walls; those yellow and white lines you see painted on the playground for when we play sports; his mop.

- Dislikes: Pigeons, mice, rats or any other living creature that might spoil the look of the school; oh, and raisins (for obvious reasons).

- Grumpiness level: 10 (out of 10)

- Other interesting facts: I think he prefers the school when there aren't any children in it – probably because then there's no one around to mess it up. I know this because I had to come into school once during half-term, when I'd left my coat behind, and I saw him singing ABBA songs and dancing with his broom! It was the first time I'd ever seen him looking happy.

When I arrived home that night, I got straight into practising baking my biscuits. And they were good enough that we even had them for pudding. Mum, Dad and Gran seemed to think they were OK, and nobody died from eating them, so I took that as a good sign.

Max didn't like them, though. I decided to find out why, because I thought any feedback might give me an edge in the competition – even if it was from Max.

'Why don't you like the biscuits then, Max?' I asked.

'Because they're not cheesecake,' he said.

Now, while I didn't find his feedback as helpful as I'd hoped, I couldn't fault his ability to spot when something wasn't a cheesecake.

Chapter 12

It was Thursday morning – the day of the first round of the baking competition. And even though I'd managed to fit another practice bake in the night before, I was still REALLY nervous. I was even more nervous than the time I went in a dodgem car with Max at a funfair and let him drive!

There were three groups in the opening round. The first two had taken place on Tuesday and Wednesday, and I was in the last group to go. My group included Oscar, Blake Hartley, and, of course, Cleo Hawkins. We also had a couple of kids from the other Year 6 class, another from Year 5, and a boy from Year 3. Only the top four bakers from each group would go through to the semi-finals, so if I messed it up in the first round, I'd be out.

I hadn't heard much about what had happened in the first two groups, apart from the fact that Ben Crawley from Year 5 had turned up at school that morning with a bandage on his hand. There was a rumour going around that he'd accidentally baked his hand into a pie, but I was fairly sure you couldn't bake your hand into a pie. And anyway, I knew it couldn't be true because we weren't due to do pies until the semi-final!

All the bakers had arrived at school that morning carrying an assortment of plastic containers and carrier bags full of their ingredients and kitchen equipment. Blake Hartley had brought in so much that he could barely carry it all. He had five MASSIVE carrier bags overflowing with stuff, including two pineapples, a coconut, and a giant wooden spoon that was big enough to paddle a boat with.

'It's a recipe I came up with myself,' he boasted as he tripped and smashed his way down the corridor with his carrier bags jangling. 'I call them my Tropicalé Carnivalé Cookies.'

I shuddered to think what that was going to involve. I was pretty sure it wasn't going to be as fun as it sounded, though. Suddenly, I was less worried about getting through to the next round and more concerned with getting out of the kitchen alive. If this situation had been expressed as a maths equation, it would be:

Blake Hartley + oven = giant explosion.

I seriously considered grabbing a wastepaper bin and wearing it on my head for protection. Of course, the downside of that plan was that I wouldn't be able to see anything I was doing. On the other hand, maybe not being able to see what I was doing might actually IMPROVE my baking. It certainly couldn't get any worse. I hoped!

Once I'd stashed my ingredients in the cloakroom, I tried to stop thinking about the competition, so I didn't get too nervous. And I was doing a pretty good job of distracting myself until morning break when I saw Oscar had smuggled some of the chocolate chips for his cookies out in his pocket and was slipping a few into his mouth every few minutes.

'Is that a good idea?' I asked, trying not to sound too much like a parent or a teacher. 'What is it you're baking?'

'Triple choc chip cookies,' he mumbled through a mouthful of... well, triple choc chips.

'And how are you going to make them without any choc chips?' Amrita asked.

As Oscar continued to chew, a quizzical expression crept across his face as if it was the first time he'd ever considered it might be a problem. This is fairly typical of Oscar. He's very enthusiastic but tends not to think things through. After less than a second of thinking about it, he started smiling.

'I'm sure it'll be fine,' he said. 'Want some?' He offered his outstretched hand to us. There were dozens of slightly melted choc chips stuck to his palm.

'Thanks,' I said, taking three or four. They may have looked a bit battered, but I never say no to chocolate.

He then turned to Amrita and held out his hand.

'What about you, Amrita?'

'Er, no thanks,' she squeaked, clearly horrified at the thought of eating something that had been in Oscar's pocket all morning.

The choc chips were now oozing slightly from the heat of his hand and were covered in enough fluff that you could have knitted a SCARF from them. Amrita did her trademark shudder as she stared at them.

At that moment, Blake Hartley suddenly appeared on the scene.

'Fancy a choc, Blake?' Oscar asked.

'No thanks, I've got icing sugar.'

That's right. Blake Hartley had stuffed his pockets with ICING SUGAR and was now eating it! This was bizarre behaviour even by his usual standards. Although I guess it would have been a lot more difficult to fit some of his other ingredients into his trouser pockets. The pineapples would have been particularly tricky!

We stood and watched as he shoved his ink-stained hand into his pocket and pulled out a big handful of icing sugar.

'Icing sugar, anyone?'

Amrita just grimaced and took a step back. 'You do know that you're just eating handfuls of powdered sugar, don't you?' she said. 'It's meant to be used to decorate cakes.'

Blake glanced at his handful of icing sugar. 'Does that mean that you don't want any then?'

Amrita shook her head and shuddered again.

'What about you, Cordie?' said Blake.

'No, thanks,' I replied. 'I'm fine for icing sugar.'

'It makes a great snack,' he suggested.

'What you have there isn't a snack,' I said. 'What you have is an ingredient.'

'What, you don't like icing sugar?'

'No. I do like icing sugar. I just like it mixed with water and spread artistically over the top of a delicious cake.'

It was at this point that I began to wonder whether Blake had done some sort of deal with the companies who make icing sugar to try to convince people to eat it raw. I imagined what the TV ads would look like. Probably something like this...

Blake appears holding a plain cake, then turns to speak to the camera.

Blake: 'Tired of having to go to all the trouble of baking something before you can eat icing sugar? Then stop!'

He throws the cake over his shoulder and starts walking towards the camera.

Blake: 'Why waste your time with all that pointless baking when you can have icing sugar as a tasty on-the-go snack?'

He reaches into his pocket and pulls out a handful of icing sugar.

Blake: 'Raw icing sugar provides all the sugary goodness you could want without the hassle of having to make it into actual icing. So, if you don't mind looking a bit weird – and losing all your teeth by the time you're twenty – why not try icing sugar?'

He then smiles into the camera, opens his mouth, and shoves a huge handful of the icing sugar in.

Anyway, he was just about to have another go at convincing me that eating handfuls of icing sugar was an exciting new treat when I noticed that the 'football boys' had accidentally kicked their ball over in our direction. It had landed right at Oscar's feet.

'Uh-oh,' said Oscar, staring at it like a startled racoon.

You see, Oscar is definitely not what you'd call a football boy. It's just not his thing. Oscar's into creative things like drawing and writing. He even carries a little notebook in his pocket to doodle in or write down ideas. Also, as he's got such long limbs, when he kicks the ball he can be a bit uncoordinated.

'I look like a giraffe on roller skates,' he often says. 'And not just any giraffe either – one with no previous skating experience!'

Come to think of it, maybe that's how he came up with the idea for the giraffe cake!

All eyes were now on Oscar to see what he would do next. For a split second, I thought he was going to run off, but he'd clearly decided that would look even weirder than the roller-skating giraffe thing. So, bravely, he pulled his long spindly leg back and kicked the ball as hard as he could in the direction of the football boys.

It was actually quite a reasonable attempt at a kick, but as he flung his foot at the ball, his slip-on shoe flew off and followed the ball at high speed up and across the playground. Long after the football had arrived safely back with the football boys, the shoe continued its trajectory until it flopped limply down onto someone's back like a distressed HADDOCK. And that someone was CLEO HAWKINS!

'Oh no,' I said. 'This doesn't look good.'

Cleo swung around and looked angrily across the playground. When she saw us standing there and noticed that Oscar was only wearing one shoe, she glared at us menacingly.

'Yes, Cordie,' said Amrita, 'this doesn't look good at all.'

'Aren't you going to go and get it back?' I asked Oscar, who by now was just standing there staring at his sock.

'No. Not just yet,' he said, trying to sound casual.

'But you've only got one shoe on.'

'So?' he answered. He said this as though spending the day with only one shoe on was the most normal thing in the world, and we were a couple of weird two-shoed freaks.

'But your sock's on the ground,' said Amrita; 'you'll catch something nasty.'

'I'll hop,' said Oscar.

The thought of having to spend the rest of the day with a hopping Oscar wearing a sock covered in flapjack was more than I could take. I decided I was just going to have to be brave and head over to Cleo and her sidekicks and get the shoe back. But just as I was about to set off, an object came scuttling towards us from the direction of the football boys and landed with a plop at Oscar's feet. It was back. The football boys had returned the shoe to its rightful owner, proving once and for all that those football boys will kick anything!

Oscar casually slipped it back on, as if there hadn't been a problem in the first place, and then popped another couple of choc chips into his mouth. But, unfortunately, that wasn't the end of it. Cleo and her crew were heading in our direction and she was carrying her coat out in front of her like it was evidence found at a crime scene. And even from where we were standing, we could see a big, fat, muddy footprint in the middle of the coat.

'Don't worry, Oscar,' I said. 'I'll do the talking, if you like? She already hates me.'

But just in the nick of time, the bell went for the end of break and we managed to slip into the crowd as it headed off down the path and back into the school building. We knew this wouldn't be the end of it, though. Cleo wasn't going to let this one go.

Chapter 13

After break, we had maths with Mrs Savage, the deputy head. Once a week Mrs Savage takes each of the Year 6 classes for maths. This is because she has a brain like a COMPUTER and is a brilliant maths teacher. And Mr Pip seems quite happy about this arrangement, mainly because he gets an hour off – which he probably spends sitting in the staffroom eating biscuits.

The only problem is she's VERY strict. She's so strict that she once gave someone a lunchtime detention for breathing too loudly, so we knew we couldn't risk being late for her class.

When we arrived in the classroom, Cleo was already sitting in her usual seat. I remembered thinking at the time that this seemed a bit odd. She usually stayed in the cloakroom until the very last minute, chatting to her cronies and adjusting her ENORMOUS bow.

Once everyone was sitting down, Mrs Savage started her usual routine of scanning the classroom suspiciously for any signs that we were up to no good. I'm not sure why, but she seems to think ALL children are ALWAYS secretly planning something dodgy. But this time she turned and looked at each of us carefully. It was as if she was looking for something very specific.

I began to worry that Cleo may have told her about the flying shoe incident, and that the three of us were about to get in BIG trouble. And then I started to wonder how Mrs Savage would even be able to deal with that situation. Usually, the teacher would send you to Mrs Savage's office. But she couldn't send us to see Mrs Savage, because she IS Mrs Savage. And anyway, she wasn't in her office; she was HERE with US!

What was she going to do, whiz past us in the corridor to get to her office before us? I guess she could try, but then technically, she would have had to tell herself off for running in the corridor!

I had no idea what was going to happen next, but we were about to find out.

'If I find that anyone here has been eating their ingredients for this afternoon's baking,' she bellowed, 'they'll be eliminated from the competition immediately!'

Phew, I thought, *that's a relief. She's just trying to flush out the secret ingredient eaters.*

Blake Hartley hurriedly tried to dust the icing sugar off his trousers, but he just ended up making things worse by leaving smudgy white handprints all over them.

When I looked across at Oscar, he turned to me and absent-mindedly smiled. I could immediately see that we had a HUGE problem. His teeth were covered in dark brown chocolaty blobs. He looked like one of those witches you see in little children's picture books. I gestured to him to close his mouth, but he just looked confused and smiled an even bigger smile. I knew that if Mrs Savage saw his teeth, Oscar would be thrown out of the baking competition for sure.

Just as I was wondering what I could do to get him out of his chocolaty mess, Cleo put her hand up to try and attract Mrs Savage's attention.

'Mrs Savage,' she bleated, 'somebody's stolen my rubber.'

This was just the chance I needed to warn Oscar. While Mrs Savage was distracted, I passed him a piece of paper with the following note written on it:

> Do not smile.
> Chocolate in teeth.
> You look like a mad witch.

'How do you know you haven't just lost it?' Mrs Savage barked at Cleo.

'It was in my desk before break,' said Cleo, trying her hardest to sound like a wounded puppy.

As Mrs Savage interrogated Cleo, Oscar read the note, and then hurriedly used his grubbiest finger as a toothbrush to try and destroy the chocolaty evidence.

'Could everyone please look in their desks for Cleo's rubber,' said Mrs Savage. 'And let me remind you, anyone caught stealing will face severe consequences.'

And we knew she wasn't joking. She once gave Temi Adebayo a detention because his pencil kept breaking!

For the next few seconds, there was a low buzz of noise as everyone busily searched for the missing rubber. But the hunt was suddenly interrupted by the sound of Oscar's voice.

'What's this?' he said, sounding very confused.

'What is it, Oscar?' snapped Mrs Savage.

'I don't know,' said Oscar. 'It looks like a weird rubbery donkey with an ice-cream cone sticking out of its head.'

The whole class fell about laughing.

'That's my unicorn rubber,' said Cleo. 'That's it!'

'What's it doing in my desk?' said Oscar innocently.

'Quiet!' bellowed Mrs Savage, trying to regain control of the classroom. 'Oscar, you'd better have a really good explanation for why Cleo's rubber is in your desk.'

As he handed the rubbery donkey thing back to Cleo, Oscar looked utterly baffled. Cleo, on the other hand, was doing her best to look like a complete innocent, but I was sure I could detect the faint outline of a smile in the corner of her mouth. Could it be that she'd planted that rubber in Oscar's desk to get him back for the flying-shoe incident? If she had, and Mrs Savage decided he had stolen the rubber, Oscar would be out of the baking competition for sure!

But then a truly wonderful thing happened. Blake Hartley sneezed. And the force of the sneeze caused a HUGE cloud of icing sugar to explode out of his pockets. It went EVERYWHERE, completely engulfing his entire row along with a couple of the kids in the row directly in front of him. When the dust settled, it looked like a scene from some kind of zombie movie. At least six kids were a powdery white colour and Blake, who took the biggest hit, looked like an Abominable Snowman.

Mrs Savage, on the other hand, wasn't at all white. No, she was bright red – with RAGE. She glared at the Zombie/Abominable Snow-children, looking as if she was about to explode.

'Right!' she bellowed. 'Will all the affected children go to the toilets and clean themselves up NOW!'

As they all stood up, the icing sugar plumed out into the air again, and the classroom started to look like a strange sugary snow globe. It was then that Amrita put her hand up and pointed out to Mrs Savage that a trip to the toilets might not be such a good idea.

'But, Mrs Savage,' she said, 'they'll have to go outside to get to the toilets, and it's started raining. When the rain mixes with the icing sugar, it'll go all runny, and they'll end up being coated in icing. Like cakes!'

This infuriated Mrs Savage even more because she had to admit that Amrita was right. So, in the end, the Icing Zombie People had to sit through the entire maths lesson looking like, well, Icing Zombies. Which, to be fair, was hilarious.

The other positive thing to come out of the whole Blake Hartley's Amazing Icing Sugar Volcano, was that Mrs Savage was so distracted by it that she forgot all about the Rubberised Ice-cream-donkey Theft Incident. So Cleo's attempt to get Oscar into trouble had FAILED, and he was still in the competition. Yay!

Chapter 14

After lunch, the moment of truth finally arrived. We collected our ingredients and cooking utensils from the cloakroom and made our way to the school kitchens for round one of the baking competition. As we waited outside the kitchen door, Oscar was so excited he could hardly stand still. I, on the other hand, was so frozen with fear that the only part of me still moving was my eyes – which probably looked quite creepy. But I didn't care. All I could think about was trying to get through the first round. Gran's baking lesson had definitely helped, but I knew I still had a long way to go.

The door opened suddenly and Chef appeared, looking almost as nervous as me. But then he was about to let a group of kids into his kitchen and there was no telling what might happen.

'OK, come in, everyone,' he said. 'And don't touch anything!'

I took a deep breath and we all filed into the kitchen. It was such a WEIRD experience being in the school kitchen. I'd only ever seen into it from the other side of the hatch before, and it all looked so different from inside.

The first thing I noticed was the faint whiff of today's lunch, which in my case was something called Mediterranean Hotpot. See if you can guess what was in that! The other thing that struck me about the kitchen was that nearly everything was made of metal, even the work surfaces. It made it feel a bit like being on a submarine. Not that I've ever been on a submarine – we usually take the ferry whenever we go on holiday to France!

Within seconds of walking in, I spotted THE MOST ENORMOUS POTATO MASHER I have ever seen. You couldn't really miss it because it was so much bigger than all the other utensils. At first, it made me laugh. But I soon stopped laughing when I realised that this oversized kitchen implement was the reason I was served ridiculously large amounts of mash for lunch every day. So it wasn't an amusing, bigger than usual, kitchen implement after all. It was, in fact, my MORTAL ENEMY!

As I tried to come to terms with the giant evil potato masher, I noticed Blake Hartley was standing in the doorway. I couldn't believe it! Mrs Savage was letting him take part in the competition even after the whole Abominable Zombie Icing Sugar Children Incident!

'OK, find yourselves a baking space,' shouted Chef, as we all milled around.

Chef quickly scurried over to the potato masher with an anxious look on his face.

'And keep away from the potato masher. It's a very expensive piece of equipment.'

He then patted it with the same affection that Gran pats Mr Wallace on the head!

When I first heard Chef was going to be one of the judges for the competition, I have to admit I was a bit surprised. I couldn't help wondering whether a man who only ever seemed to cook roasted vegetables, sausages and industrial-sized quantities of mash was qualified to judge a baking competition. Also, rumour has it he doesn't even eat his own cooking, and that he prefers to have a microwave meal for his lunch instead!

Maybe when he found out that Blake Hartley was in the competition, he'd insisted on being there to make sure his precious kitchen didn't get blown up!

The second judge was my form teacher, Mr Pip, and it was no surprise he'd volunteered. His eating abilities are legendary. He's constantly snacking throughout the day, and the way he can eat an entire school lunch in less than five minutes is truly impressive. And the packed lunch he brings on school trips is so big that it won't fit in the overhead luggage racks on the coach!

It was time to settle in, so we all found a place around the worktops and unloaded our bags of ingredients and equipment. I was on a table with Oscar, Cleo, a kid from Year 3 and Blake (oops-I've-just-made-something-go-on-fire) Hartley.

The kid from Year 3 looked really young. He was so small for his age that he had to stand on a box to reach the work surface. I wasn't going to underestimate him, though. He had some pretty fancy equipment, which included his own hand-held electric whisk! He also had a cake-splattered notebook that he clung to as if it contained the secret to the universe. And he really seemed to know his stuff. He kept going on about something called chocolate ganache? I had no idea what that was, but it sounded like a rash you might get from eating too much chocolate. I crossed my fingers and hoped I didn't get it!

I had Oscar standing on my left, which was a big relief because it meant we could give each other some support. And diagonally across from me was Cleo, who was wearing a purple apron with the words 'Perfect Princess' written on it in swirly pink glitter. I, on the other hand, was wearing an apron with a cartoon kangaroo on it that Gran found in a charity shop. The kangaroo had a speech bubble saying, 'G'Day Mate!' which I think is Australian for hello. Oh, and it had wonky eyes, which made it look completely crazy.

I was also massively relieved to find Blake Hartley was right down at the other end from me. The way I looked at it, at least then we'd get a chance to see the explosion coming and be able to dive under something before we were engulfed in a huge thunderball of cake batter!

As we were organising our ingredients on the work surface, Oscar leant across to me with a worried look on his face.

'Uh-oh!' he whispered.

'What?'

'I think I may have eaten too many choc chips and now I don't have enough left for my cookies.'

'How many do you have left?' I asked.

He looked into the various carrier bags scattered on the work surface in front of him.

'Erm, let's see,' he said, rifling through his bags again.

I was pretty sure by now that I knew what was coming next. Eventually, he turned to me with a confused look on his face.

'None,' he said, looking as if they had all just disappeared by magic.

'How many do you need for the recipe?'

'Fifty grams.'

'Yeah, I can just about manage that,' I said. 'I was going to melt mine and drizzle them over my almond and honey cookies, but I'll skip that and you can have them instead.'

'Thanks soooo much, Cordie!'

'Maybe try not to eat them between now and when we start baking in a few seconds' time,' I said chuckling.

Oscar was still looking worried.

'Anything else?' I asked, praying that the answer was no.

'Fifty grams of sugar,' he muttered apologetically.

'You ate the sugar?'

'I got hungry.'

'But you've just had lunch. And anyway, sugar isn't a snack.'

'Well, it's just that I thought Blake Hartley made a good point about the whole icing sugar thing, and so I thought I'd see if the same applied to ordinary sugar.'

He looked at me blankly and shrugged, as if the whole thing was not under his control.

'Here, you can have this. I'll just use slightly less.'

I passed him the sugar and choc chips, hoping he didn't need anything else. For a few seconds he just stared at the floor, looking really guilty.

'Are you sure?' he asked. 'I don't want to mess things up for you.'

'Yeah, it's fine,' I said. 'I don't think the world's quite ready for your triple choc chip free cookies made without any of the basic ingredients needed to make triple choc chip cookies.'

To be honest, it wasn't entirely alright. I was already worried about my chances even with all the ingredients, so I could have done without having to give some away. But it was Oscar who was asking. He was one of my best friends, and that's what best friends do.

And with that, Mr Pip announced that we had forty-five minutes to bake our entry. And we were off...

Chapter 15

The first twenty minutes seemed to go by in a flash. The Year 3 kid, or 'Jake the Cake' as I decided to call him, was off to a flying start. He was working so quickly that he honestly looked like he had twelve arms. And he was so focused that he reminded me of a NASA astronaut, although I doubted there were any astronauts who had to stand on a booster step to reach the controls of the rocket!

Things weren't off to such a great start for Oscar, though. He was so overexcited that after a few minutes he'd already managed to poke himself in the eye with a spoon. Twice!

And when I looked up a bit later, his hair was covered in butter. But Oscar's problems were nothing compared with what was going on over the other side of the work surface.

Watching Blake Hartley bake was like watching a duck learn to play the piano. He spent the first ten minutes attempting to smash open a coconut with his giant wooden spoon. But every time he hit it, the coconut shot across the work surface and scuttled over the edge onto the floor. To be honest, he didn't even look like he was in a baking competition. He looked like he was competing in a really weird game of golf with some kind of giant, hairy brown egg. And knowing Blake Hartley, it wouldn't be long before he claimed he'd invented an exciting new game. He'd probably call it something like Hairy Egg Whack!

Blake's antics were in stark contrast to Cleo. She looked like she really knew what she was doing. As long as she didn't accidentally set her MEGA BOW on fire, she was bound to go through to the next round.

Before I knew it, we all had our biscuits in the oven and we were sitting on the floor looking in through the oven doors.

As we counted down the last few minutes before our biscuits came out of the oven, Oscar revealed to me that he'd decided to make a last-minute change to his cookie recipe.

'Well, as you know,' he said, trying to sound casual, 'originally I was going to make triple choc chip cookies.'

He was looking at the floor and nervously pushing some discarded sugar back and forth with his foot, so I suspected there was a problem.

'But then I decided that, you know, you can have too much chocolate. So, I thought I'd go with double choc.'

'Right,' I said.

'And then I thought double choc chip might be confusing because that's not really a thing. So, in the end, I decided to go with straightforward, classic single choc chip.'

'OKaaaaay,' I said, knowing something bigger was coming.

'But then right at the last minute,' he said, by now in a really squeaky voice, 'I suddenly thought, you know what, the judges may not even LIKE chocolate, so why not leave it out altogether.'

'So, you ate all the choc chips then?' I said wearily.

'Yeah,' he said, trying desperately not to make eye contact with me.

Before I had a chance to say anything else, Mr Pip told us we only had three minutes left before we needed to get our biscuits out of the oven. My heart started to race. I was REALLY worried about mine. The mixture didn't look anything like it had when I practised making them at home. It was hard to say whether it was because I'd given Oscar some of my ingredients, or whether I'd just messed up spectacularly. I stared at the oven door, just hoping it wouldn't be a total disaster.

'Right, that's it,' Mr Pip shouted. 'Time's up, everyone. Take your bakes out of the oven and place them on the judging table.'

I took a deep breath and prepared to face my fate. Was my challenge to Cleo Hawkins the masterstroke of a brave genius, or the reckless move of the kind of idiot who sleeps on a landing with a stinky dog who's known by his surname? Deep down, I thought I probably already knew the answer.

One thing was certain though, if I didn't get through the first round, I would lose the forfeit and have to get up and sing in front of the entire school. And to make matters worse, the whole thing would have been my idea. Those biscuits HAD to be OK, or I'd never be able to live this down.

Chapter 16

It was the moment of truth. I knew that only four people from our group would go through to the semi-finals. And, deep down, I didn't think I had much chance of being one of them. Everyone else looked like they actually knew what they were doing – apart from Blake Hartley, obviously. And Oscar would have been in with a chance too, if he hadn't eaten half his ingredients.

When I first put my biscuits in the oven – which took ages because I couldn't work out how to open the oven door – I wasn't even sure they would come out as biscuits. And when I peeked in at them halfway through the baking time, I thought they looked more like weird knobbly pancakes.

But when I took them out of the oven, I was REALLY shocked. At first, I thought there'd been a mix-up, and I'd accidentally taken out somebody else's. But they were mine, and to my amazement, they actually looked like biscuits!

I carried my tray over to the judging table, trying hard not to drop them all. Could it be, I thought to myself, was it possible... could I dare to dream that they might even taste like biscuits, too?

We all waited nervously for the judges to start the tasting. And now, with my biscuits that looked like ACTUAL BISCUITS, I began to feel that I might be in with a chance.

'OK,' said Chef, standing in front of the judging table. 'Mr Pip and I will sample your bakes, then we'll take ourselves off for a private conversation where we'll decide which of you goes through to the next round. Good luck, everyone. You've all done very well.'

There were three kids on the other table and one of them, Amelia from Year 5, looked like she was definitely a contender. Hers looked really good. Better than mine, if I'm honest. They were more of a cookie than a biscuit and were much bigger and more succulent looking.

'Right, let's start with these cinnamon and sultana cookies,' said Chef, picking up one of Amelia's cookies and breaking it in half. 'It's got a lovely texture inside.'

Mr Pip nodded in agreement and took a big bite. But within a few seconds, he suddenly stopped chewing and put the rest of the cookie back on the plate. Everyone was in a state of shock. We'd never seen Mr Pip turn down food before! What could possibly be so awful that Mr Pip found it unacceptable to eat?

It didn't take Chef long to work out that Amelia had accidentally used CURRY POWDER instead of cinnamon and, without meaning to, had introduced Mr Pip to a whole new world of flavour. And just like that, the curried sultana cookie was born!

'Yes, that was a nice try, Amelia,' said Mr Pip. 'But I think you might need to do a bit more work on your flavours.'

'I agree,' said Chef, looking VERY relieved that it was Mr Pip who'd tried it and not him.

When it was my turn to have my biscuits tasted, I was so nervous that I couldn't watch. And when I dared to open one eye, I half expected to see the judges staggering around, clutching at their throats and pleading for someone to call an ambulance. But I couldn't have been more wrong.

Instead, they were nodding and even making 'yummy' noises.

'Very good,' said Chef, enthusiastically, which I thought must be a good sign considering there wasn't even any mash in them!

Mr Pip grunted his approval too, before quickly shoving another one into his mouth.

I couldn't believe it! Whenever I'd baked them at home, they'd never been quite right. But these were obviously pretty good. Maybe in a strange, weird way giving Oscar some of my ingredients had actually improved them.

Once Chef and Mr Pip had worked their way through all the entries, they took themselves off to a quiet spot over by Chef's precious potato masher to make their decision.

As we waited for the results, my mind drifted. Chef seemed so attached to his giant potato masher; I began to wonder if he ever daydreamed about it. Perhaps he fantasised about taking it on one of those TV talent shows. I'm not sure what their act would be? Just mashing stuff, I guess?

Finally, Chef and Mr Pip finished their discussions and stepped forward to make their announcement.

'OK,' said Chef. 'There have been some excellent bakes here today, but here are the four bakers who will be going through to the semi-finals. Firstly, these ginger biscuits.'

He pointed to the biscuits that had been made by the kid from Year 3, Jake the Cake. I wasn't surprised. I had tried one of them and they were like golden discs of gingery perfection.

'Well done, Jake,' said Mr Pip. 'They were scrumptious.'

'These were excellent as well,' said Chef, pointing to the entry from Little Miss Perfect Cleo. I couldn't face trying one of hers, but they looked, well, perfect.

As I waited anxiously for the verdict on mine, Cleo gave me a weird kind of look. A thin smile crept across her face, and I knew instantly what she was thinking. She was probably imagining me singing badly in front of the entire school, while trying desperately to distract people from my awful voice by wafting my arms around like a windmill.

There were only two places left in the next round. I swallowed hard and crossed all my fingers behind my back.

'And these were also delicious,' said Mr Pip, holding up a plate of MY cookies. 'So, well done, Cordelia, you go through to the semi-finals, too!'

He then picked up another one of my biscuits and put it into his mouth whole.

When I'd recovered from the shock of getting through to the semi-finals, I glanced over at Cleo. She looked furious.

And she wasn't the only one who was furious. Looking out of the window, I noticed Mr Bugler shaking his fist and shouting at a bemused-looking pigeon. The poor bird, who was casually sitting on top of the fence, clearly hadn't seen his sign that read 'Strictly NO Leaning on the Fence'.

Back in the kitchen, Oscar's triple chocolate chip cookies didn't go down too well with the judges. With no chocolate in them – because he'd eaten it all – he crashed out of the competition. Although that didn't stop Mr Pip from eating FIVE, before deciding that they weren't very nice.

'Sorry, Oscar,' I said. 'I hope you're not too disappointed.'

'Thanks, Cordie,' he replied. 'I'm not really surprised, though. And it's been a pretty good day overall.'

'In what way?' I asked.

'Well,' he said, 'it's not often you get to spend the entire school day stuffing your mouth with chocolate chips.'

This was so typical of Oscar. No matter what happens, he always looks on the bright side.

'And anyway,' he continued, 'I've also learnt an important thing about myself.'

'What's that?' I asked.

'I think I like snacking.'

So that was it. Oscar had discovered something about himself that the rest of us already knew. And, in other news, I was through to the semi-final, which meant that I was one step nearer to beating Cleo Hawkins, and one step further away from having to humiliate myself in school assembly. Oh, and let's not forget, I'd also survived being in a kitchen where Blake Hartley was using an oven. Now that really was amazing!

Oh yes, I nearly forgot to mention who also got through. After not being able to crack the coconut open, Blake Hartley compensated by putting pineapple juice into his cookie mix! And as the mixture cooked, it spread out over the entire surface of the baking sheet to form one giant cookie. But, against all the odds, the judges thought the flavour was fantastic and that the idea of a giant cookie was really fun and different. So, Blake made it through to the semi-finals!

I think it was fair to say that everyone was in shock. Except Blake, of course, who thinks everything he does is

BRILLIANT. You've got to hand it to that kid – he always manages to pull something out of the bag. And this time it was a pineapple!

Anyway, he was so hyped about getting through that he decided to travel back to the classroom using his baking tray as some kind of not-very-good skateboard. Unfortunately for him, he collided with Mrs Savage and ended up getting himself a detention. Classic Blake Hartley!

Chapter 17

That evening, as we all sat around the dinner table, I was still buzzing from getting through the first round of the baking competition.

'Well done, Cordie,' said Mum. 'You really deserve it after all the practising you've been doing.'

'I knew you could do it, Cordie!' said Gran.

'Yes, that's great!' said Dad. 'I've been checking my phone all day, waiting for a call from the Fire Brigade.'

'I thought I could smell burning at school today,' said my brother, flashing a smile at Dad because they'd both made a joke about my baking.

Mum seemed genuinely pleased for me, though.

'I don't know where you get your baking talent from,' she said, 'but it certainly isn't me.'

'You got that right,' chuckled Dad, which earned him a glare from Mum.

'Anyway,' said Gran, quickly changing the subject, 'what are you going to be cooking in the next round, Cordie?'

'Well, funnily enough, I'm going to be doing pastry,' I said, 'and I'm really worried because I've never actually made pastry before.'

'Well, don't worry, Cordie,' trilled Gran. 'I'll teach you all my secrets for baking perfect pastry. We can start tomorrow night if you like?'

'Thanks, Gran,' I said. 'I need all the help I can get.'

At this point, my little brother piped up. He hadn't been getting any attention for a whole five minutes, so he'd clearly decided he needed to get in on the action.

'Actually, I've got some pretty big news too,' he announced.

'Really?' I said, rolling my eyes. 'Let me guess, is it mashed-potato related?'

'No.'

'Hamster related?'

I could tell instantly that it was because he looked really irritated that I'd guessed right.

'Well, yes, but...'

'Oooo, how exciting,' said Gran, trying to encourage him. 'What is it, Max?'

'I've been teaching Colin a trick!'

'A trick?' I said. 'He's a hamster, not a dog. You can't train a hamster.'

'Wanna bet?!' said my brother.

Before I could respond, he picked up a bemused-looking Colin, put him on the table and placed Mum's phone down about fifty centimetres in front of him.

'Hey, what are you doing with my phone?' said Mum. 'I need that for work.'

But she was too late. Max was already dangling a sunflower seed at the other side of the phone, trying to tempt Colin forward with his favourite crunchy treat. It was all the motivation his furry friend needed. With his whiskers twitching frantically, Colin sped across the kitchen table, leapt into the air and landed with a big SPLAT on top of Mum's phone.

It was at precisely this moment that Grandma's phone started ringing at the other side of the room. She got up and scuttled over to the kitchen counter where her ENORMOUS bag sat slumped in the corner. And after rummaging around inside it for what felt like several weeks, she finally managed to find her phone.

'Hello,' she said, holding the phone awkwardly to her ear.

When she didn't hear anything, she thought it might help if she spoke a lot louder.

'Hello!' she bellowed. 'I can't hear you. Could you speak up, please?'

'Gran, I think...'

'Yes, hang on, Cordie dear,' she said. 'I'll be with you in a minute. I'm just taking a call.'

Of course, the rest of us noticed straight away that Colin's splat landing on Mum's phone had accidentally pressed Gran's number in her Contacts.

'I don't think there's anyone there, Mum,' she said. 'It's not a real call...'

But Gran was determined not to give up.

'All I can hear is a strange scratching sound,' she said.

'Gran, I think Colin...'

'Colin? Colin who?' said Gran. 'Hang on, I can hear something now. It's a bit squeaky, though. Could you speak up please, Colin? You're quite squeaky at this end.'

By now, everyone was desperately trying not to laugh, while Gran attempted to make herself understood by shouting down the phone. And the more she shouted, the funnier it got. Finally, Dad decided to put her out of her misery.

'Grandma,' he boomed, 'you're on the phone to a rodent.'

Gran swung around just in time to see Colin prancing about on top of Mum's phone, squeaking away with delight.

'Oh,' said Gran, chuckling away to herself. 'Well, look at that. I thought it was the builders!'

Whether my little brother was prepared to admit it or not, it was clear that Colin the Amazing Flying Hamster wasn't quite ready to headline at the O2 Arena.

It was also clear that I wasn't ready for the next round of the baking competition. I'd never baked pastry before, and if I didn't learn before the semi-final, I'd have to sing in front of the whole school. The social humiliation would be epic. It would be like being raisined times 1000!

Let me be clear about this, I am VERY BAD at singing. I sound a lot like a DUCK trapped in a WASHING MACHINE. And please don't ask me how I know what a duck trapped in a washing machine sounds like – I just do!

The last time I appeared on stage was at a Christmas carol concert, and during one of the carols, everyone got a turn to sing a line solo. Mine did NOT go well. Just as the person before me was finishing their line, I realised that I was about to unleash a massive burp!

I tried desperately to swallow the burp down, but there simply wasn't time. This meant that the first few words of my line were burped. The last few words were normal (in a duck trapped in a washing machine kind of way) but, unfortunately, I sang them in the wrong order, so they sounded like gibberish. Then, at the end of singing our line, we were supposed to sweep our arm across in front of us towards the person who was singing the next line. Simple enough, right? WRONG! When I did it, I put too much swing into it and knocked Lucas Manning off the edge of the stage.

So, to the horrified teachers and parents in the audience, it looked like I'd burped my way through a carol before attacking one of my classmates. How Christmassy!

All of this meant it was CRUCIAL that I did everything I could to avoid having to sing in front of the school. The semi-final was only a few days away and everything was now resting on Gran's pastry masterclass. I just had to hope she'd have something up her sleeve other than a banana.

Chapter 18

When we arrived at school on Friday morning, I was HORRIFIED to discover that there was a display of photos just inside the main entrance showing the highlights of the first round of the baking competition.

Of course, my brother didn't waste any time in letting me know the good news.

'Hey, Cordie,' he bellowed. 'Isn't that a photo of you?'

As everyone looked around to see what the commotion was, I glared at him with my best mum-style glare.

I walked over to the display, cringing with embarrassment. There I was for the WHOLE school to see, wearing my bizarre kangaroo apron and holding a plate of biscuits. But hang on a minute... my face was gone. Well, it hadn't gone exactly. It had been replaced by a gigantic bow.

'Why is your face a bow?' asked my puzzled brother.

In the photo, Cleo was standing next to me and she was leaning in at such an extreme angle that her bow pretty much blocked out my entire face.

'Because I'm standing next to Cleo – the girl with the biggest bow in the world, that's why,' I replied.

Was it deliberate? Probably. Did I care? No, because it meant that I was less recognisable in the photo. So, without realising it, she'd actually done me a favour.

Next to the photos, there was a sheet of paper pinned up, giving details of the draw for the semi-finals. My heart did a little somersault when I discovered Cleo Hawkins was in a different group from me!

And the good news just kept coming. The first semi-final was due to take place on Monday afternoon, which meant that I'd miss PE! I couldn't remember the last time a school day had started this well. I felt like punching the air in celebration, but decided against it because it might have looked a bit odd and I was already on shaky ground with my weird kangaroo apron.

At morning break, Amrita told us that it was her birthday in a few weeks' time, and that this year she was going to have a party. This was quite big news because Amrita doesn't usually have a birthday party – mainly because she can never decide on a theme.

Obviously, Amrita won't have anything to do with insects, yucky stuff, or WIGWAMS – so they're all out. And she's not that keen on anything too dangerous either, which means climbing up things, jumping off things, or flinging yourself about is also off the agenda.

Since wigwam parties aren't a huge thing (as far as I know), they're fairly easy to avoid. But ruling out all the other stuff was going to seriously narrow down the party options.

The amazing thing about Amrita is that she's perfectly happy to do things that most of us would hide under a desk to avoid – like get up on stage in front of hundreds of people and give a speech or even sing a solo in the choir! I guess she's clever enough to know that she's unlikely to come across any of the things she hates while she's doing it. Let's just hope she's never asked to give a speech about wigwams near an open window and a swarm of FLYING SPIDERS swoop in and she accidentally falls off the stage in shock!

Anyway, as Gran said recently, we all have quirks. At least I think that's what she said. It was difficult to understand what she was saying because she was eating a banana at the time!

So, for Amrita, planning a birthday party was going to be a huge task. Basically, it would have to meet all her requirements but still be fun (i.e., not be held in a library). This was NOT going to be easy.

'So let me know if you have any ideas,' Amrita said.

'What about bowling?' suggested Oscar.

'No. It's too much of a verruca risk for my liking.'

'A verruca risk?'

'From the bowling shoes,' said Amrita, shuddering as she thought of having to wear the same shoes that dozens of other people had already worn.

'What about swimming, then?' said Oscar, determined not to give up.

'No, there's the deep end,' said Amrita, her eyes widening.

'A picnic?'

'Wasp attack,' said Amrita.

'A pizza-making party?'

'People not washing their hands.'

'How about a standing still party?' I quipped, trying to lighten the mood.

Amrita's eyes lit up, and for a moment she looked almost enthusiastic. 'How would that work, exactly?' she asked.

Before I could answer, the bell went for the end of break.

'Hang on a minute,' she said. 'You just made that up, didn't you?'

'Yeah,' I said.

'That's a shame,' she said with a big smile on her face. 'I think I'd have really enjoyed a standing still party.'

As we headed back into class, we joked around about what a standing still party would look like. But then I noticed Oscar had stopped laughing and had an unusually serious look on his face.

'What's up?' I asked.

'Oh nothing,' he replied. 'Only, I just remembered that I'm going away this weekend with my sister and my dad.'

'That's nice,' I said, trying to sound encouraging.

Oscar turned to me, looking grim-faced and worried.

'It's a bushcraft weekend, Cordie.'

'Uh-oh,' I said, borrowing Oscar's catchphrase for a moment, and knowing he was going to find this about as much fun as sports day.

I understood completely – I wasn't the outdoorsy type either. And Amrita definitely wasn't.

Unlike Oscar, his dad and his older sister are VERY outdoorsy. They climb up stuff and jump over stuff and run a lot.

'I'm so gangly and uncoordinated,' said Oscar, 'that when I run, I feel like I'm on a bouncy castle!'

'Well, you're still quicker than me!' I said.

He looked at me gloomily. 'And we're sleeping in yurts!'

'In yaks!?' said Amrita, who'd only been half listening because she was probably still daydreaming about having a lovely birthday party where everyone just stood still.

'Yurts,' repeated Oscar.

Amrita looked horrified and was no doubt already imagining what sleeping inside a YAK would mean from a hygiene point of view.

'What's a yurt then?' I asked.

'I dunno,' said Oscar. 'I think it's some kind of weirdy tent thing.'

'Oh no!' said Amrita. 'That sounds suspiciously like a wigwam to me.'

'Dad said this weekend will be the making of us – the three of us living out in the woods for a couple of days. But I can't help thinking about all the twigs and things I'll trip over with my long, wobbly legs. And imagine trying to survive in the wild with these.'

He wiggled his spindly arms right under my nose.

'That's literally my worst nightmare,' said Amrita.

'What, my arms?'

'No, camping. Imagine all the flying spiders. In fact, that's probably where most of them live! You poor thing, Oscar.'

'Look on the bright side,' I said. 'At least it's only for a couple of nights. And by the time you get back, Amrita might have even decided on her party theme.'

'No chance,' said Amrita, chuckling.

And I knew she was right. This party was going to take some serious planning.

Chapter 19

When I arrived home from school that night, I could hear Gran clattering about in the kitchen, setting things up for our pastry-making masterclass. It was the next round of the baking competition on Monday, so I needed to do lots of practising over the weekend to be in with a chance, and I couldn't wait to get started.

Mum wasn't quite so enthusiastic, though. You see, Gran is a brilliantly funny, easy-going and kind person. In fact, you couldn't wish for a nicer gran. But she can be quite disorganised and a bit haphazard. So having Gran in the kitchen making pastry wasn't exactly Mum's idea of a relaxing evening.

I passed Mum in the hall and she looked at me despairingly.

'I suppose it's for a good cause,' she said. But she had a look on her face of somebody who knew there was a fair chance she'd be deep cleaning the kitchen at midnight. And that was only if things went well. If they went badly, she'd be redecorating it!

Before I could say anything, we heard a huge crash from the kitchen that made us both jump. Mum took a deep breath and sighed.

'It sounds like there's a herd of cattle stampeding through there,' she said.

'Don't worry, Mum. We'll just send Mr Wallace in to lick the kitchen clean when we're finished.'

This made us both laugh.

'Go on then,' said Mum. 'I guess it's going to happen anyway, so you may as well get changed.'

When I reached the top of the stairs, I noticed a sign on my brother's bedroom door that read:

'NO ENTRY. HAMSTER TRAINING IN PROGRESS.'

I was desperate to find out what was going on, so I pressed my ear up against the door. On the other side, I could hear my brother's voice BELLOWING out orders like he was some sort of animal trainer at the CIRCUS. I couldn't believe what I was hearing. I actually started to feel a bit sorry for Colin Hargreaves. It seemed like a lot to have to go through for a shrivelled old sunflower seed. I could only think that he must REALLY like them. It made me wonder whether I could train Max up in the same way by dangling some sausage and mash in front of him. It had to be worth a try!

But all that was going to have to wait. I quickly changed into some old clothes (as a precaution) and hurried back downstairs for my pastry-making masterclass with Gran. But when I reached the kitchen, I realised I wasn't the only one who'd changed. Gran appeared to be wearing what can only be described as some sort of KARATE UNIFORM!

'Er, Gran,' I said, as I looked her weird outfit up and down.

'Oh, hello, dear,' she answered. 'I didn't see you there. Are you ready, then?'

'What are you wearing?'

'Oh this,' she said, adjusting her HEADBAND. 'This is what I wear when I bake pastry, dear.'

'But why?'

'What you have to realise is that pastry making is an ancient art that goes back centuries. So, it's very important to treat it as a discipline and clear your mind of all distractions. It's only then that you can develop your "pastry focus".'

As she said this, she tapped the side of her forehead with her index finger.

Now, as much as I love Gran, her talk about 'pastry focus' still didn't explain why she was standing in our kitchen dressed like she was about to compete in a martial arts competition.

But she wasn't finished with her speech.

'To make the perfect pastry,' she continued, 'you need to connect with the pastry; you have to understand the pastry.'

'OKaaaay,' I said, still wondering whether this was all a joke.

'You and the pastry must be as one,' she said in a strange 'floaty' voice. It was like the voices you hear in dream sequences on TV or in a film, but it was Gran saying it and she was standing in my kitchen dressed like a karate teacher. So, obviously, I struggled to take it seriously.

'So just to recap,' I said, trying not to laugh. 'You think my best chance of getting through to the next round of the baking competition is if I BECOME a pie. Is it enough that I think I'm a pie, or do I have to actually get into the pie?'

'I can see this isn't going to be easy,' said Gran calmly. 'I had exactly the same problem with your mother when she was your age.'

'What, so she didn't want to become a pie either?' I said, grinning.

'She wasn't prepared to connect with the pastry,' replied Gran patiently.

I began to realise from the look in her eye and her tone of voice that Gran was DEADLY serious about this, so I decided I'd better go along with it. After all, I really needed the help, and it suddenly occurred to me that it might be quite fun making pastry with a KARATE MASTER.

'Alright then,' said Gran. 'So, I thought we'd practise by making a nice banana pie together. Then, maybe over the weekend you could have a go at making one on your own.'

What a surprise, I thought. We were only ten seconds in and Gran had already managed to involve bananas. And

I was pretty sure I had never even heard of a banana pie, either.

But once the lesson had started, all my doubts disappeared as I saw my loveable, daffy gran turn into some kind of pastry GRANDMASTER. It was such a weird experience watching her in action. She had the laser focus of an assassin, or should that be ninja? I looked on, mesmerised, as she went through her well-rehearsed process. It was like being in the presence of a PASTRY SUPERHERO.

When it came to the part where she had to mix the flour and the butter together, she called for complete silence as she closed her eyes and allowed her fingers to work their magic.

'You'll know when the pastry is ready,' she said. 'You can tell by the touch.'

Once the pie was in the oven, she took off her headband and my lovely normal gran reappeared. It was like she had come out of a trance and was now herself again. I couldn't tell which version of her I liked the best, my loveable old gran or Pastry Woman.

The weirdest thing was that even though the whole process had seemed really precise and calm, when I looked around the kitchen, it was like a scene from a disaster movie. It was as though we'd been concentrating so much on the pastry-making process that neither of us had noticed the mess that was piling up around us. I guess it was like being in the eye of a storm.

Apparently, the very centre of the storm is eerily calm. It's the outer edges that create all the damage. It seemed strange to think of Gran as being a hazardous force of nature. I began to imagine what the weather warning for this might sound like.

(Serious newsreader type voice)
This is an urgent weather warning.
Gran will be passing through the local area on Friday.
Residents are advised to stay indoors for their own safety.
It is expected that Gran will cause widespread damage, including rail and road closures and disruption to power supplies. Oh, and watch out for flying bananas.

OK, so maybe I'd gone too far. Gran wasn't really a devastating natural phenomenon that could cause wide-scale destruction. And then I remembered her botched DIY attempts and realised that I might be right after all.

Despite the mess we'd created in the kitchen, the pie turned out to be really yummy! I'd never come across a banana pie before, but this one was lip-smackingly delicious. Right there and then I decided that I would be making a banana pie in the semi-final. Karate Gran had really come through for me. And later that evening I even helped Dad to clean up the kitchen, so everyone was happy!

On Sunday we had another baking session, and I made the pie myself with Gran supervising. I didn't put on a karate outfit for the occasion, but I did wrap a school tie around my head just to show Gran that I was prepared to 'connect with the pastry'. I then carried out her instructions to the letter, even closing my eyes when it was time to mix in the butter. And do you know what? The pie turned out to be pretty good. Even Max ate some. In fact, it went down so well that he was too busy eating it to think of anything sarcastic to say!

Chapter 20

It was Monday – the day of my semi-final. And after a weekend of pie-baking practice, I'd started to believe that I might actually be able to bake a fairly decent pie. My sessions with Gran had given me a real boost, so I was feeling upbeat when I bumped into Oscar and Amrita in the cloakroom.

Unfortunately, Oscar and Amrita weren't feeling quite as cheery. Amrita was no closer to deciding on a party theme, and it was beginning to drive her mad. And Oscar had made a very important decision. He was definitely NOT a bushcraft kind of guy.

Of course, anyone who'd ever seen Oscar do anything physical could have told you that BEFORE he went on the bushcraft weekend from hell. But just in case we were in any doubt at all, he'd come back with a BROKEN ARM!

'Oh, Oscar, you poor thing,' said Amrita. 'What happened?'

'If you don't mind, I'd rather not talk about it,' he muttered. 'I don't really want to relive the whole thing. Let's just say it occurred during an "outdoor incident".'

Of course, we assumed this meant he had been swinging on a rope over a fast-flowing river, or trekking up the side of a treacherously steep mountain. But the truth was a little less impressive. After a bit of coaxing, he finally admitted that he'd actually broken it by slipping on a discarded SAUSAGE near the campfire!

'They're cooked in oil,' he protested. 'They're very slippery. It could have happened to anyone.'

Poor old Oscar. Some people just aren't built for the great outdoors, especially when it's a bit too sausagey.

I hung the bags with all my ingredients and equipment in the cloakroom and tried to put the semi-final out of my mind. But the longer the day went on, the more nervous I became about the horror I'd be facing if I lost.

And speaking of horrors, as we came out of the classroom just before morning break, I bumped into Cleo in the corridor. She was as confident as ever.

'Looking forward to your semi-final, Cordie?' she purred.

'Can't wait,' I said, lying through my teeth, determined not to let my nervousness show.

'What are you going to burn this time?' she chuckled, making her cohorts laugh as they shuffled off down the corridor.

I didn't stay focused on Cleo for very long, though, because I was so distracted by what I saw next. It was Jake the Cake. And there was something alarmingly different about him. He looked taller. A LOT taller. How was that possible? It had been less than a week since I'd last seen him, but he'd clearly had an EPIC growth spurt in the meantime.

Of course, a sudden growth spurt is something that can happen to anyone. My brother once went up three shoe sizes in a month, and by the third visit to the shoe shop, Mum couldn't take it anymore.

'It's getting so expensive buying you new shoes,' she said, 'if your feet grow again, we'll just have to send you to school in Dad's flip-flops.'

The strangest thing about it was that she didn't say this to Max. She said it to his FEET. I don't know what she was expecting to happen. Did she think the threat of having to turn up to school in Dad's bizarre rainbow effect flip-flops would be enough to persuade the feet to see sense and stop growing? Was she hoping they wouldn't want to run the risk of being socially embarrassed in front of all the other feet?

Ever since then, whenever I see Mum staring at the ground, deep in thought, I wonder whether she's thinking about some sort of secret 'foot world' that exists. Like a parallel universe – but for feet.

As everyone piled into the cloakroom to get their morning snacks, I shuffled in nervously and looked down at MY feet. I wondered if they knew they would be taking part in the semi-final of a baking competition later that day. And, if they did, what did they think our chances were? And I was just about to ask them, when I realised that talking to my own feet was probably a sign that the pressure of the contest had got to me.

I grabbed my ingredients bag off the coat hook and began rummaging around in there for my morning snack – a banana, obviously! But as soon as I put my hand inside something felt wrong. VERY wrong. In a gloopy kind of a way. I quickly pulled my hand back out and looked at it in horror. It was covered in some kind of gluey substance.

When I reluctantly opened the bag and peered inside, I found the stalks of four bananas. Mr Wallace had struck again! And this time, not only had he eaten my morning snack, he'd also eaten the filling for the pie I was planning to bake in the SEMI-FINAL! What was I going to do now? There was no way I could bake a banana pie without bananas.

'What's up?' said Amrita.

'Slight problem,' I said, trying not to freak out. 'Mr Wallace has eaten the main ingredient of the pie I'm supposed to be baking this afternoon. And now I'll probably get knocked out of the competition, which means Cleo Hawkins will have beaten me, and I'll have to get up and sing in front of the whole school.'

Amrita looked stunned.

'Mr Wallace, the substitute teacher, ate your bananas!?'

'What's happened?' said Oscar as he strolled over.

'Mr Wallace, the substitute teacher, has eaten the bananas Cordie was going to use in the baking competition,' said Amrita, shaking her head in disbelief.

'No way! Why would Mr Wallace, the substitute teacher, eat your bananas?' said Oscar, far too loudly.

'OK. Everybody calm down,' I said. 'Mr Wallace, the substitute teacher, did not eat my bananas. Mr Wallace, my grandmother's dog, has eaten my bananas.'

To be honest, I was having trouble staying calm myself. I was about to compete in the semi-final of a baking contest without the main ingredient of my bake, and my two best friends couldn't grasp a simple piece of information about Mr Wallace and some missing bananas.

Oscar looked a bit puzzled, and I could immediately tell what was coming next.

'Who gives a dog a surname?' he said.

No doubt about it, it was an excellent question. But I simply didn't have time to explain the STRANGENESS that is my family. So, I pretended I didn't hear the question, and pleaded with Oscar and Amrita to help.

'What am I going to do?' I said. 'I won't be allowed to go home and get more bananas, and now I don't have a filling for my pie.'

'OK,' said Amrita, suddenly taking charge. 'Let's approach this logically. Oscar, what did you bring for snack time?'

'An apple. Why?'

'Ah ha! Me too! Now, let's see what else we can dig up.'

As word went around the cloakroom, lots of people started to offer up their morning snacks to help me out. In the end, I managed to get:

- two apples;

- a flapjack;

- a small pot of strawberry flavoured custard;

- some fizzy sweets;

- and stringy cheese.

Admittedly, it was an unusual collection of stuff, but I was really grateful.

'Thanks so much, guys,' I said. 'I really appreciate it.'

But the truth was, I needed more than two apples to be able to make an apple pie, so I was still in trouble. And I wasn't entirely convinced about the stringy cheese either!

My pastry was going to have to be quite spectacular for me to survive this.

The good news was that at least I had some options for my filling. The bad news was that there was now a rumour going round the school that our substitute teacher Mr Wallace had eaten all my bananas.

Chapter 21

At the end of the lunch break, Oscar and Amrita wished me luck and headed off to their afternoon lessons. I took a deep breath and made my way to the cloakroom to collect my strange pie ingredients.

As I stood outside the kitchen waiting to go in, I was horrified – no, make that terrified – to find that I had ended up in the same group as Blake Hartley again. So not only did I have to win my place in the final with the weirdest pie ingredients since Gran last baked one of her 'pastry pies', but I also had to try to stay alive in a kitchen where Blake Hartley was doing things with an oven!

Jake the Cake was also in my group, but there was no need for him to use a step to reach the countertop this time. Since his epic growth spurt, he was now the size of a Yeti (only not as hairy, and not an actual Yeti or anything) and towered over everyone else.

I looked around at the other competitors. Nobody looked as nervous as me. But then nobody else was about to make a pie out of string cheese and chewy sweets.

The other three contestants in our semi-final were a mixed bunch. There were two girls from Year 5, who seemed to be good friends. And there was a boy from Year 4, who had a confused look on his face as if he wasn't sure why he was even there.

To be honest, I was just relieved that I was in a different group from Cleo. At least I'd be able to see what I was doing without the shadow cast by her GINORMOUS bow!

Chef pulled the door open, and we all filed in.

'Find yourself a space around the worktops,' he shouted, gesturing to his freshly cleaned kitchen. 'And get all your stuff out, so you're ready to bake.'

While we got ourselves organised, I couldn't help but notice Mr Pip's eyes staring hungrily at all the ingredients laid out on the work surface. Chef, on the other hand, was busy watching Blake Hartley; clearly worried that if he took his eyes off him for even a second, the kitchen would probably explode.

And, suddenly, it was time to start. Mr Pip took out his watch and prepared to give us the countdown.

'OK, contestants,' he shouted. 'Is everyone ready? You have an hour and a half to bake your pies. Good luck! Five, four, three, two, one. Bake!'

I grabbed my ingredients for the pastry and started mixing them together, but it wasn't long before I started to FREAK OUT. The pastry was going all wrong. First it was too crumbly; so I added more water. Then it was too wet; so I added more flour. But when I tried to roll it out, it was far too crumbly again and bits kept breaking off. It wasn't anything like it was when I did it with Gran.

Then, just as I felt like giving up, an image of Gran dressed in her karate uniform appeared in my head. Mr Wallace (the dog, not the substitute teacher) was standing by her side eating a banana. Gran spoke to me in an echoey voice like she had before.

'Be at one with the pastry,' she said. 'Trust the pastry.' And with that, Gran and Mr Wallace (still the dog and not the substitute teacher) went all wobbly and disappeared.

Pulling myself together, I thought back to Gran's baking lesson at the weekend. And then I suddenly remembered, I needed to put the pastry in the fridge to let it rest for a while before rolling it out. Of course! Gran told me that doing this allowed something to happen to the gluten in the flour and made it easier to roll out! Either that or maybe the pastry just gets really tired from all the mixing and needs a bit of a lie-down. I'm not sure which.

Anyway, while the pastry was having a nap in the fridge, I started to look at the ingredients I had for the filling. This was going to be a tricky decision. I agonised for ages, trying to work out what would be the least awful combination. But as I did, I got more and more worked up until, before I knew what was happening, I just threw everything into the bowl together!

I don't know what came over me. I guess the pressure of the contest finally got to me and I panicked. I stood there, frozen to the spot.

'Oh no, what have I done?' I whispered to myself.

Taking a deep breath, I peered into the bowl. There I found diced apple, crumbled flapjacks, fizzy sweets, strawberry custard and stringy cheese all bobbing about together like a really, really WEIRD soup.

But there was no turning back now. I just had to get on with the next stage. So, I took the pastry out of the fridge and woke it up from its nap. Then I rolled it out and placed it carefully in the pie tin, just like Gran had shown me. Next, I tumbled the strange fruity-creamy-crumbly-fizzy-stringy mixture into the pie case. And finally, I gently lowered the pastry lid onto the top. Everything was ready. There was nothing more I could do. I turned the oven to the right temperature and slipped the pie inside. It was now up to the pastry gods.

As for my fellow semi-finalists, Jake the Cake made the whole thing look ridiculously easy. Even though he was now the size of a Yeti, he was still as calm and focused as ever – constantly checking his trusty notebook and whizzing around at top speed like a pro. In fact, he was finished so early that while his pie was in the oven, he had time to make some custard FROM SCRATCH to go with the pie!

Blake Hartley, on the other hand, was making the whole thing look like a CAR CRASH. He'd been eating his ingredients throughout the bake, and it was difficult to see how he was going to be able to make anything out of what he had left that could reasonably be described as a pie.

Of course, none of this was surprising. It was standard Blake Hartley stuff. One thing that DID surprise me though was how low-key he'd been while he was baking. Normally, he'd have given a running commentary on everything he was doing in a big, booming voice, only ever stopping to laugh at his own jokes. But this time, he was quiet. Too quiet. I was convinced he was up to something.

'You have five minutes left, bakers,' shouted Chef, 'so your pies should be almost ready.'

I peered into the oven at my pie and began to wonder how I'd managed to get caught up in this ridiculous situation in the first place. It was simple. I'd allowed Cleo to wind me up, and then challenged her to a baking competition, even though I knew she was really good at baking. That was almost as stupid as letting Blake Hartley loose in a kitchen. But it was way too late to change the past. The baking time was almost up and we had to get the pies out of the oven.

'OK, bakers,' shouted Mr Pip. 'Please take your pies out of the oven and bring them over here to the judging table.'

Chapter 22

Not surprisingly, Jake the Cake's apple pie looked PERFECT! The pastry was bronzed and glistening in a way that made you wonder if it had actual glitter on it – although I'm fairly sure it didn't. And the filling! WOW! It had a beautiful golden lake of apple and cinnamon oozing from underneath its gloriously flaky crust. It was a masterpiece, and Chef seemed to agree.

'Excellent,' he said. 'A first-class pie.' He dipped a spoon into the custard and tried a mouthful, then nodded his approval.

And as for Mr Pip, by the time he'd finished his slice he was looking so dazzled by it, I thought we might have to build a fence around what was left of the pie to stop him from finishing it.

I glanced down nervously at my pie. The pastry was a nice golden colour and, from the outside at least, the pie looked quite appetising. The big question was whether the judges would appreciate the CHEESY FIZZINESS of the filling. I thought about it for a while. The odds weren't good. I based this on the fact that I had never heard anyone say the words 'cheesy' and 'fizzy' in a good way, particularly when talking about food.

'OK,' said Chef. 'Let's try this next one.'

As the judges bit into my pie, I closed one eye and crossed my fingers.

'The pastry is excellent,' said Chef, 'exceptionally light and crisp.' Then his expression changed. 'The filling on the other hand...'

Uh-oh, I thought, borrowing Oscar's catchphrase again.

'... the filling is a really interesting contrast. I can't quite place it. What is it?'

I opened my eye and tried to speak. 'It's a secret family recipe,' I squeaked.

'Well, it's very unusual.' There was a big pause while he stared into space and let his taste buds do their work. 'And very good.'

'Yef, it's bevry pasty,' muttered Mr Pip through a mouthful of pie, before helping himself to a second portion.

I couldn't believe it. They actually liked my pie! I knew the pastry would probably be OK, but somehow the filling hadn't made them throw up all over the kitchen. It was like some kind of baking miracle!

Next, the judges tasted the two Year 5 girls' pies. The girls were clearly best friends, and had worked side by side throughout the bake, like a synchronised swimming team. They had both made identical-looking pear and almond pies. And the pies looked pretty good, so they were definitely competition. But it turned out I didn't need to worry. One of them had forgotten to put the filling in the pie, and the other girl had copied her because she wanted to be the same. Chef looked confused and Mr Pip looked disappointed – although he did still eat the pastry.

When the girls realised what had happened, they didn't seem too upset. I guess it was better for their friendship than if one of them had gone through to the final and the other had been left behind.

Then it was time for Blake Hartley's pie to be judged. I don't know whether it was just my imagination, but as Chef hovered over it with the knife, it felt like everyone took a step back.

It just looked so weird. It looked more like a hat than a pie. But it was what lay beneath the pastry that was really worrying. It had a disturbingly knobbly appearance, unlike any pie I'd ever seen before. Chef looked equally worried as he cut into it, which was actually quite tricky because it was as hard as a ROCK in the middle. When they eventually did manage to break through the crust of the 'Hat Pie', it quickly became obvious why Blake Hartley had been so quiet while we were baking. Blake Hartley had baked a CALCULATOR into his pie!

'Why would you do that?' asked Chef, shaking his head and looking even more confused than the confused-looking boy from Year 4.

'I ran out of ingredients, and anyway, there's nothing in the rules that said I had to use food as a filling,' said Blake defiantly.

But there was no point in questioning him about why he'd done it. The truth is not even Blake Hartley knows why Blake Hartley does the things he does. And that's what makes Blake Hartley Blake Hartley. I hope that clears things up!

Anyway, obviously this meant that he was out of the running. Not even Mr Pip tried any.

The confused-looking boy's pie was the last to be tasted. He'd looked baffled throughout the bake, and even seemed surprised when he opened the oven door to find he'd baked a pie. I don't know what he'd been expecting, since he'd put an unbaked pie into it about an hour earlier. And when the judges cut into it, he seemed genuinely shocked to see it was a cherry pie!

After the judges had finished tasting, they gathered in a huddle for a few minutes – although it felt like much longer. Eventually, they came over to announce the winners.

'The three winning pies are...' said Chef, 'the apple pie with custard, the cherry pie and the pie with the unusual filling!'

Jake the Cake looked fairly happy, in a relaxed sort of way. I was smiling so hard that my teeth probably looked like they were about to fly out of my head. And the confused-looking boy from Year 4 looked – well – confused.

The last I saw of him that day, he was walking down the corridor scratching his head as if he didn't know what had just happened. I wondered how he'd managed to enter a baking competition and get through two rounds without knowing why he was there. I guess it was quite an accomplishment, really.

As it sank in that I had made it through another round of the competition, I closed my eyes and silently thanked Team Cordie for all their support. Thank you, pastry gods! Thank you, Karate Gran! Thank you, friends who gave up all their weird break-time snacks!

I gathered up my things and started to leave. As I did, I could hear Blake Hartley's voice as he complained to the judges about their decision.

'I can't believe you haven't sent me through to the final,' said Blake. 'If anything, I should get extra points for trying something different. I've basically invented a new type of food.'

'And what would that be?' said Chef, probably grateful that all his teeth were still intact.

'A Numbers Pie,' said Blake. 'It's so versatile. You can eat some pie and do your maths homework all at the same time.'

I had to smile. So, Blake Hartley thought he was an inventor, did he? Well, as long as he wasn't sticking a piece of mouldy dried fruit down the back of my coat and screaming RAISIN at the top of his voice, I wished him well.

So, I was through to the final. I couldn't wait to tell Oscar and Amrita. I also couldn't wait for Cleo to find out I'd made it through. She wouldn't be able to believe it! I couldn't believe it either. I was still in the competition and there was still a chance that I could avoid the humiliation of having to sing a solo in front of a traumatised-looking school.

As school days go, it had been a pretty good one.

Chapter 23

When I arrived home from school that evening, Gran was waiting for me at the door. She was THRILLED when I told her that I'd made it through to the final, and after she'd given me a big hug, she stood there and smiled her widest smile. She had a knowing look in her eye, like she'd been expecting it all along. I guess for Pastry Woman, it was just another successful mission. You know, like James Bond, but flakier... and without the helicopter.

Mum was really pleased for me, too.

'So, what did the judges say about the banana pie?' asked Gran. 'I'll bet they couldn't eat it quickly enough, could they?'

'Well, unfortunately I didn't get to use the bananas you gave me for the filling,' I replied, 'because when I opened my backpack, only the stalks were left.'

'Oh no! How did that happen?' said Mum.

'Well, I can't say for certain, but the stalks were covered in the teeth marks of someone who isn't too far away from where we're standing right now.'

'Max?' asked Gran, clearly puzzled as to why my little brother would have broken into my backpack and eaten bananas with their skins on.

'No, Gran, someone hairier.'

'Your mother?'

'No, Gran,' I said, trying not to laugh as I noticed the look of annoyance on Mum's face. The suggestion she was well known for being HAIRY clearly hadn't gone down well.

'Let me give you a clue,' I said. 'He's got a tail.'

I looked at Mr Wallace and furrowed my brow, but he just wandered over to me and sniffed my pockets as if he was looking for more bananas.

'Oh,' said Gran, suddenly realising who I was talking about. 'Sorry about that, Cordie. I'm afraid he does love his bananas.'

'Yes, and everybody else's,' I joked.

'So what did you put in the pie?' asked Mum.

I told them about Oscar and Amrita giving me their snacks, and the other kids in the cloakroom chipping in to make the weird filling that I ended up with.

'And did it still taste OK?' Mum asked with her face screwed up at the thought of my cheese fizz pie.

'Apparently,' I said. 'The judges thought it was unusual but very tasty.'

'It's that pastry,' said Gran. 'You could put anything in there and it would still be delicious.'

'Yes,' I said, smiling back at her, 'anything apart from a calculator.'

That night, after I'd recovered from the shock of my fizzy, fruity, cheesy pie's victory – and the horror of Blake Hartley's Numbers Pie – I started to plan what I was going to bake in the final. When I found out the following day that Cleo had also made it through, I decided I'd have to up my game.

I pretty much spent EVERY EVENING that week practising baking my cake for the final. And after a few days, nobody in our house wanted to eat another crumb of cake. Except for Mr Wallace, of course, who wanted to eat the entire cake followed by the plate the cake was on, and then the table the plate with the cake was on. I could keep going, but you get the idea.

I didn't see much of Max that week, as he spent most of the time in his bedroom. He claimed he was teaching Colin a new trick that would astound the world. I told him that teaching a hamster ANY trick would astound the world, but he just shook his head dismissively and shut his bedroom door again.

Gran had been due to go back to her house once the builders had replaced the wall, but halfway through the week Mum announced that she was going to be staying for a bit longer. When she broke the news to me, I was helping her clear up the dinner plates, which was to make up for the fact that I'd pretty much broken the kitchen with all my practice baking. I could tell she hadn't been looking forward to telling me.

'I'm sorry, Cordie,' she said, 'but it won't be for too much longer.'

Apparently, while the builders were working in the house, they discovered that Gran had carried out some 'experimental' plumbing in the kitchen. And when they turned up on the last morning to finish off the wall, they found the kitchen had flooded.

'Oh yes, it does that,' said Gran, when Mum asked her about it. 'I think I may need to change the way I've arranged the pipes.'

The weird thing was she said it as though she was a professional plumber with twenty years' experience, but I'm not sure the plumbers would have agreed.

So, anyway, Mum decided that Gran couldn't go back to the house until she was sure that the builders had made it safe, which meant that she'd be staying with us for a few more days. Unfortunately, so would Hairy McFarty Pants the incredible gas-powered dog.

Chapter 24

When I woke up on the day before the final, my nerves had already started to kick in. On our way into school, my brother decided to tell me about his hamster-related plans for world domination. He does this most mornings, and it usually drives me nuts, but this time it actually helped because it took my mind off the competition.

While Mum was a few paces behind us, taking a call from work, Max was in full flow on his plans for Colin.

'And then we'll probably go on a world tour,' he said.

'Right,' I said.

'And then, when we've finished that, I expect we'll get some sort of call from the United Nations, and they'll ask Colin to help them out.'

'Really?' I said. 'The United Nations? Do you mean like a United Nations Peace Envoy or something?'

'Yep.'

'Sorry, but don't UN Peace Envoys travel to areas in the world where wars are raging and try to stop them?' I asked in disbelief.

'That's right,' replied my brother confidently.

'And you think Colin, your hamster Colin, WHO IS A HAMSTER, would be an ideal candidate for that role?'

'Why not?'

I could think of a million reasons why not: the main one being that COLIN IS A HAMSTER! But I knew from past conversations that if I said that, he'd just accuse me of being anti-hamster. So instead, I just shook my head and replied, 'No reason,' and we trudged on.

As we got closer to the school, I tried to amuse myself by imagining a press conference with Colin outside the United Nations headquarters. The world's press would all be there, as Colin, wearing a tiny suit over his hamster fur, announced via a series of squeaks and twitches how he had managed to stop another war.

But the moment I walked through the school gates, my nerves came back when I saw Cleo's gigantic bow bobbing along ahead of me. I started to think about tomorrow's final again, and what I would be facing if I lost.

Why, oh why, had I chosen singing as a forfeit? I could have chosen anything, anything! What about dancing? Dancing would have been great.

It was then I remembered, I'M A TERRIBLE DANCER, TOO!

In fact, the only thing I seem to be good at is thinking of things that Cleo isn't very good at and then realising I'M NO GOOD AT THEM EITHER!

The image of me up on stage singing badly in front of the whole school kept flashing into my mind for the rest of the morning, and I found it really hard to focus on anything else. In science, we were learning about the earth's atmosphere and Mr Pip must have noticed that I was staring out of the window.

'So, Cordie,' he said. 'What are the main constituents of air?'

I was so distracted that I answered without thinking, 'A hundred and fifty grams of flour and a beaten egg.'

The whole class fell about laughing. Blake Hartley was laughing so hard that he claimed he couldn't breathe.

'Stop,' he said, barely able to speak. 'I can't breathe. It's probably because of all the flour and eggs in the atmosphere!'

As he stumbled around, gasping theatrically, the class collapsed into fits of laughter again.

At lunchtime, there was some sort of hold up in the kitchen and we had to queue up outside before they could let us into the lunch hall. But when Mr Bugler, the caretaker, came past and saw us waiting there, he went mad at us because we were leaning against the wall.

'Stay away from that wall,' he grumbled as he walked away. 'I don't want you lot ruining it with your arms.'

I'm not quite sure why Mr Bugler thinks that ARMS could RUIN walls, but it seemed pretty unlikely to me. If that was the case, surely we'd have heard something about it by now. For a start, wouldn't there be warning signs up on all walls?

Warning! Leaning on this wall could make the building go splat.

OK, maybe not that precise wording, but something like that, only more adult sounding and grumpy.

I was just thinking what a ridiculous thing this had been to say, even for Mr Bugler, when I glanced down the line and saw Blake Hartley's arms. They were covered in something green and smooshy. OK, so they weren't going to make the wall collapse – although I guess you could never rule out anything with Blake – but they were certainly going to leave a mess.

It was a mystery how Blake had managed to get green stuff on him during the morning. He'd been in all the same places as the rest of us, but somehow, he'd discovered a hidden supply of green stuff and rubbed it all over his arms.

It was then that I realised for the first time that Blake Hartley wasn't the unruly character we all thought he was. He was actually very reliable because you could ALWAYS depend on him to do something REALLY stupid.

Chapter 25

When we arrived home from school at the end of the day, Mr Wallace greeted us in his usual overenthusiastic way by snuffling and snorting around at our pockets. Getting through the door of our house was now a bit like going through customs at the airport. Mr Wallace, the permanently hungry dog, seemed to be on a personal mission to stop anyone smuggling 'illegal' sausages or other food into the house.

So, before letting us enter, he would 'search' us all. Presumably, if he found anything, his next move would be to take it away for 'testing'. Although I'm pretty sure his version of testing would have involved a lot of chompy, chompy and nom, nom, nom.

I suppose if you're a dog, it would be easy to believe that humans only ever leave the house to hunt for sausages, which we then carry home by stuffing in our pockets and socks. But as we struggled through the door and shook off the rain, Max wasn't in the mood to be lick-searched by a dog.

'Get off, Mr Wallace,' he bellowed, pushing him aside and racing up the stairs.

'Have you got any homework?' Mum called after him.

'Yes, but I'll do it later. I've got a practice session scheduled with Colin at 4 p.m., and I don't want to keep him waiting.'

'No, of course not,' I said. 'Colin has a very busy schedule. FOR A HAMSTER!'

Mum and I went out to the kitchen to join Gran, but it wasn't long before we began to hear a lot of banging and crashing coming from upstairs. It sounded like half a dozen HIPPOS at a Zumba class. Then, the crashing noise suddenly stopped, and we heard my brother shouting out in a panic.

'Oh no! Colin!'

He burst out of his bedroom and sprinted down the stairs, looking like he'd just found out there was a national mash shortage and from now on, everyone would only be allowed one portion of mash a week. But what had actually happened turned out to be far, far worse.

'Colin's missing!' he shouted at Mum. 'The door of his cage is open and I can't find him anywhere.'

All the stomping around we'd heard had been Max turning his bedroom upside down to look for Colin. So it wasn't a hippo Zumba class after all – which was a shame because that would have been very cool. But there was no time to daydream about hippos in leotards exercising to music. Max needed my help.

For the next hour or so we searched every corner of the house while being followed by an overexcited Mr Wallace. In his big hairy dog brain, he'd probably mistaken all the commotion for some sort of 'find the pork pie' game.

The longer the search went on, the more I started to worry that perhaps Mr Wallace didn't really need any more food because he'd already eaten. Could it be that he'd discovered Max's hamster friend earlier and decided that it was chompy-chompy time for Colin? I decided it was probably best to keep that theory to myself for now. Max was already freaked out enough.

As the search continued, I was fairly sure Colin was still in the house, or at the very least inside Mr Wallace inside the house. But my brother soon had other ideas. He was suddenly convinced that Colin had escaped from the building.

'Don't worry, Max,' I said, trying to cheer him up. 'I don't think there's much chance of that. I mean, how would he reach the front doorknob? And even if he could, he wouldn't have got far because he doesn't have a bus pass.'

But that just made Max very angry, and Mum glared at me like she does if I accidentally laugh at Gran when she's trying to work her phone. So I decided to shut up and just keep looking for the hamster.

When Max disappeared into his bedroom and didn't come out for a while, I started to feel AWFUL about what I'd said to him. I was about to go and explain to him that I was just trying to lighten the mood when he suddenly appeared holding a handmade leaflet, which he waved at Mum desperately.

'Mum, look, I've made this,' he said. 'Can we make copies of it on the computer, so I can put them through our neighbours' letter boxes?'

The leaflet read:

Have you seen Colin?
He went missing on Thursday. He is a talented acrobat and a loyal friend.
His likes include: eating sunflower seeds, sniffing things and foreign travel.
His dislikes include: classical music, soup and rude dogs.
Oh, and he's a hamster.
A ONE MILLION POUND REWARD is being offered to anyone who can provide information leading to Colin's safe return.

And then at the bottom was our address, along with Mum's phone number.

Once she'd read the poster, Mum stopped glaring at me and started staring in horror at my little brother. It was hard to tell whether this was because of the ONE MILLION POUNDS she may have to hand over as a reward for a lost hamster, or the fact that Max was about to give her phone number out to the entire neighbourhood. On balance, I'd say it was probably a bit of both.

But she could see how panic-stricken Max was, so despite not being particularly happy about it, she agreed to make some copies of the poster. She even agreed to upload it onto her social media accounts.

'I would suggest one little change to the poster, though,' she said gently, clearly hoping that Max wouldn't explode. 'Personally, I wouldn't say how much the reward is.'

'But if we don't say how much it is, people might think it's not worth looking for Colin.'

'Maybe,' said Mum. 'Or perhaps they might think it could be a billion pounds and then they'll look even harder.'

It was a bit of a desperate move on Mum's part, and I was certain that Max wouldn't go for it, but against all the odds, he agreed. So, they quickly went upstairs to make the changes to the poster and print off some copies. Max then rushed downstairs to put on his coat, and he and Mum got ready to distribute the posters around the neighbourhood.

I was feeling a bit guilty about mocking Max's hamster training earlier, so I offered to go with him to lend a hand. And Gran said she'd come, too.

'I can take Mr Wallace for his evening walk at the same time,' she said.

When he heard this, Max looked at me panic-stricken. And I knew I'd have to come up with something quickly to persuade Gran to leave Mr Wallace at home.

'Is that a good idea, Gran?' I asked. 'Mr Wallace might not like having his walk constantly interrupted so we can stop to put up posters.'

'Yes, maybe you're right, Cordie,' she said. 'I'll take him out for a nice brisk walk once we get back.'

Max breathed a huge sigh of relief, and so did I. If we did spot Colin, it wouldn't make him any easier to catch if he saw a hungry-looking Mr Wallace bounding towards him like a BIG FURRY CROCODILE with his mouth wide open!

It was only when we were several streets away from our house that I realised we might have made the wrong decision by leaving him behind. What if Colin WAS still inside the house? If he was, he was now trapped there with Mr Wallace. But hearing this would have stressed Max out even more, so I just kept quiet and hoped it wasn't CHOMPY-CHOMPY time back at the house.

We spent about an hour pounding the streets, putting up posters and pushing them through all the letter boxes in our area. The new improved poster included a photograph of Colin, which Max said he had added just to rule out any cases of mistaken identity.

When we finally got back to the house, Mum quickly posted some stuff on her social media accounts with a photo of Colin and the bold headline of 'Have you seen this runaway hamster?'

And while we'd been out, Dad had arrived home from work and cooked us all some dinner. Max wasn't hungry, though, and went straight up to his room. Mr Wallace, on the other hand, was very, very hungry, which I took to be a good sign. Maybe he hadn't eaten Colin after all. Or maybe he had, but he considered Colin to be nothing more than a light snack.

Either way, with everything that had happened that evening, I hadn't been able to do any more practising for tomorrow's final of the baking competition. So, as I settled down on my inflatable bed later that night, I decided I would just have to trust the pastry gods and hope they were on my side.

It was then that I remembered I was baking a CAKE for the final. Did the pastry gods even cover cake, or were they strictly for pastry? Perhaps there were all sorts of different gods for different sweet treats. Maybe there was even a god of doughnuts, I thought, as I drifted off to sleep.

Seconds later, I woke up in a panic-stricken state, gasping for air. A thick, noxious cloud of gas surrounded me. I tried desperately to breathe, but the smell was like the bottom of a wheelie bin. It was so bad, I wondered whether perhaps a foreign enemy state had declared war on us during the night and had begun bombarding us with massive stink bombs while we slept!

And then I realised... it was just Mr Wallace. He'd farted AGAIN! I turned over, but as I did, I thought I heard a noise. I decided to ignore it. It was probably just the sound of yet another piece of the ozone layer breaking off thanks to Mr Wallace's nuclear farts. I held my nose and drifted back off to sleep.

Chapter 26

Before I knew it, I was back at school and standing outside the kitchen waiting to be called in for the grand final of the baking competition. As I walked nervously through the doors, I quickly realised something wasn't quite right.

Cleo Hawkins had strange wobbly arms and Jake the Cake was small again. But not the kind of small he was before his growth spurt. I mean REALLY small. When I stood next to him, it looked like I was standing next to a PEA! He wasn't green or anything he was just very, very teeny tiny.

I was just wondering how he was going to bake a three-tiered cake if he couldn't even reach his booster step, when I felt a huge SPLAT of something wet land on my head. I looked up to see where it had come from and spotted Blake Hartley floating on a giant meringue, pelting people with whipped cream and strawberries. I know he hadn't been thrilled about getting knocked out in the semi-finals, but there was no need for that!

Then, after what seemed like hours, Mrs Collins, the head teacher, appeared in the doorway. She had a giant pineapple instead of hair, and when she spoke, she sounded like a frog.

'Blake Hartley,' she croaked. 'Stop throwing strawberries and cream at Cordelia. It states quite clearly on the menu that today's pudding will be chocolate cake. I will not have you throwing the wrong pudding at my pupils. Now float off out of here and go and hover outside Mrs Savage's office.'

So Blake and his giant meringue floated off through an open window, which was great timing because it wasn't long now until our cakes would be ready to come out of the oven. I wondered what the judges would make of mine.

And that was another surprise. Mr Wallace (the dog, not the substitute teacher) was one of the judges, except he didn't look like he usually does. He was still a dog, but now he was dressed like a man in a suit with a bow tie. And he was wearing a pair of glasses. Anyway, just as I thought they were going to ask us to take our cakes out of the oven, a Key lime pie appeared out of nowhere, and we had to wait while Mr Wallace ate it and then burped out the alphabet.

Finally, it was time to present our cakes and start the judging. With Jake the Cake now the size of a pea and Cleo with her wobbly arms, I started to think I might actually be on track to win. But when I took my cake out of the oven, it didn't look very cake-like. That's because it wasn't cake at all, it was SAUSAGE AND MASH! And that's not all. The mash just kept GROWING and GROWING until we all floated off on a sea of mash. Mr Wallace tried his best to eat it as fast as he could, but even he couldn't eat it quickly enough.

'Send for reinforcements!' he shouted, sounding a lot like a cartoon dog.

Then Mr Pip appeared out of nowhere, and suddenly I was watching a mash-eating contest. It was Mr Pip against Mr Wallace, and I was one of the judges. It was like having a front-row seat at the fight of the century. They were both legends when it came to having a massive appetite, but I knew Mr Wallace would win. After all, how many chair legs has Mr Pip eaten? Compared to Mr Wallace, he was just a beginner.

When Mr Pip couldn't eat any more, Gran's insatiable dog was still chomping away, looking as though he had only just got started. And, despite all the mayhem, he was still smartly dressed in his suit, with his glasses perched on the end of his nose. Oh, and did I mention, he also had a moustache.

And then I WOKE UP. Thankfully, it had all been a dream.

Of course, as I opened my eyes, Mr Wallace was standing there, looming over me as usual. Only this time he wasn't wearing a suit, and the glasses and moustache had gone too. But he seemed just as hungry as he had been in the dream. He sniffed at my hair half-heartedly, but when he realised there was no sausage roll smell, he gave up and lay down for a nap.

Chapter 27

Nobody said much at the breakfast table the following morning. Max was still very upset about his missing hamster and was a LOT quieter than usual.

Normally at breakfast, he'd be juggling a hamster in one hand and a slice of toast in the other, and bellowing about how Colin was going to astound the world. But instead, he was just sitting there, silently pushing his uneaten cereal around with a spoon. It was unnerving to see him so quiet. I felt really sorry for him.

Mum and Dad were clearly worried about Max, too. Even though they were rushing around trying to get ready for work, they still came over every few minutes to check on him.

'Don't worry, darling,' said Mum, 'Colin will turn up soon. I'll bet someone will see one of your posters and phone us up later today.'

'Do you think so, Mum?' said Max, brightening up a little.

'Yes, I'm sure they will,' she replied.

But Mum didn't sound convincing enough for Max, and she noticed his face had fallen again.

'Let's just try to stay positive and see what the day brings, shall we?' she said encouragingly.

Max gave a sad nod.

'Now finish up your breakfast. We'll have to leave for school in a minute.'

Just then, Gran breezed into the kitchen, went straight over to Max and gave him a little kiss on the head. And for once, he didn't wipe it off. She then turned to me and gave me a big smile.

'So, it's the big day today, Cordie. Are you looking forward to the final?'

I hadn't mentioned the final so far that morning because I didn't want to take any attention away from Max. But now Gran had asked, I thought it should be OK to talk about it.

'To be honest, Gran, I'm terrified,' I said. 'I know I've baked the cake almost every night this week, but I've never managed to get it quite right.'

'You're going to be fine,' said Gran. 'Just remember, move slowly in your mind and let the ingredients work their magic.'

As she pottered around the kitchen in her slippers, Gran looked like Pastry Woman on her day off. I wondered whether Pastry Woman ever doubled up as Cake Lady. If she did, I could certainly do with some cake-making vibes coming my way before I left the house.

'I had a dream about the competition last night,' I said, 'and in the dream, Mr Wallace was one of the judges. And he was wearing a suit and a bow tie.'

'Oh no, he wouldn't like that,' said Gran, shaking her head. 'I tried a cardigan on him last winter when we had a problem with the heating and he hated it.'

'Why do you think he hated it so much?' asked Max, who'd been momentarily woken from his misery by the idea of animals in knitwear.

'Because it didn't suit him,' replied Gran.

This was such a weird statement, even by Gran's usual standards, but she hadn't finished.

'To be honest, I think he's more of a jumper kind of a dog. He has very specific tastes,' she added proudly.

If this was true, and Mr Wallace really was that fussy about what he would wear, then it was in stark contrast to his attitude towards what he was prepared to eat. In fact, he was so easy-going about what he'd eat that it didn't even have to be food!

My nerves were jangling all the way to school, and they didn't improve much when I bumped into Cleo Hawkins as we were going through the main gates. She was carrying all her ingredients in two designer carrier bags from one of those flashy shops in the shopping centre. When she saw the supermarket bags I was holding, she scoffed and shook her head dismissively.

'What have you got in there, Cordie, a ready-mix cake mixture?' Her friends all laughed as if they were already congratulating her on her victory.

'No,' I quipped back at her. 'One bag is for my ingredients, and the other is to carry the trophy home.'

Of course, this would have been a much more impressive response if my voice hadn't gone all SQUEAKY and WEIRD, so that the word 'home' came out so high that it even made me jump. As it was, they just stared back at me and then burst out laughing again.

When I reached the cloakroom, Amrita and Oscar had already arrived. Amrita could tell instantly that something was wrong.

'What's up, Cordie?' she asked.

'Oh, it's Cleo Hawkins,' I said. 'I bumped into her at the gate and she was her usual annoying self. And, as if that wasn't bad enough, my voice went weirdly squeaky for no apparent reason.'

'Don't worry, Cordie,' said Oscar, 'when you beat her in the baking final, she won't be so smug then.'

'That's the trouble,' I said. 'There's no way I'm going to beat her. I've been practising baking my cake all week, and it's never turned out right. I wish I'd never got myself involved in this stupid competition.'

But Amrita wasn't prepared to listen to any negative talk. And I knew from past experience she could be very commanding when there weren't any flying spiders around.

'Now, come on, Cordie,' she said, 'you're going to go into that kitchen this afternoon and you're going to win that competition. Don't forget, there's a lot more riding on this than who has to sing a stupid song in assembly. There are a lot of kids in this school who've been given a hard time by Cleo and her cronies, and they'd love to see you win against her.'

Amrita was right. Over the years, Cleo Hawkins had upset a lot of kids with her uppity manner, and she had got a lot more into trouble with her snitching ways. I guess I had to do it for all the kids she'd treated badly. Oh, and, obviously, I REALLY didn't want to have to sing in front of the entire school!

'OK,' I said. 'Let's do this!'

'Woo-hoo!' said Oscar, a bit too loudly. 'Those kids are going to love it when you win and put Cleo in her place once and for all!'

'Did you get all your ingredients out of the house without the dog getting hold of them this time?' asked Amrita.

'Yeah, I think so,' I said.

I opened up the carrier bags and double-checked that all my ingredients and equipment were still there. And I was just about to stash them behind my coat and try to put the competition out of my mind when I thought I could see a strange rustling coming from inside one of the bags.

'What's going on?' said Oscar, pointing at the fluttering movement. 'Have you got some sort of wind-up toy in there?'

'I don't know,' I said, genuinely mystified by the strange motion.

I slowly opened up the carrier bag and cautiously peered inside. The seconds that followed were a blur of frantic activity. There was a scratching and scurrying, and then SUDDENLY Colin the hamster's head appeared at the top of the carrier bag! But before I could grab him, he jumped down onto the cloakroom floor and disappeared out of the door and into the corridor.

'Colin, come back!' I shouted, rushing out after him, but when I reached the corridor, he was nowhere to be seen. Max's beloved pet had vanished into thin air.

'What was that?' said Oscar.

'It was my brother's hamster, Colin,' I said. 'Max has been looking for him ever since we got home from school yesterday. He must have hidden in my bag to get away from Mr Wallace.'

Oscar looked puzzled. 'The substitute teacher?'

'No,' I explained wearily, 'Gran's dog.'

Amrita looked horrified. 'So, let me get this straight. The ingredients you have in your bag have had a hamster scrabbling all over them?'

'I guess so,' I replied.

She shuddered her usual shudder. And just like that, grown-up, in control Amrita was gone, and my dear old friend 'is it on me, get it off me!' spider-hating Amrita was back. I breathed a sigh of relief. Everything had returned to normal. Except for the fact that Colin the hamster was now on the run in our school!

Chapter 28

It was hard to concentrate on anything the teachers said that morning because I was constantly checking the floor for a small, furry rodent that was now on the loose somewhere in the school.

At morning break, we knew we were in a race against time to find Colin before Mr Bugler the caretaker did. Everyone knew Mr Bugler HATED all mice and rats, as well as pigeons and squirrels. In fact, he called any small creatures he found on the school's grounds VERMIN, and they didn't get to stay on school grounds for very long.

We can always tell when he's spotted one of these dangerous intruders because we'll see him rushing down a corridor or running across the playground waving his fist and shouting, 'You're not authorised to be on school property!' I always think this is an odd thing for him to say. It makes it sound as though he would have let them stay if they'd signed in at the school office and were wearing a visitor's pass!

One thing was certain, though, Colin would definitely fall within the category of vermin, and he wasn't going to get a warm welcome from Mr Bugler.

But before we could start hunting for Colin, we had to find Max and tell him what had happened. Usually, he spent his break time hanging out with the other Year 4 boys over by the trees, but when we went to check, he wasn't there.

'He told us he wasn't in the mood,' said his friend Frankie Mason.

Eventually, we found Max sitting alone on the bench outside the kitchens, looking really miserable. But when I told him what had happened in the cloakroom, he suddenly LEAPT TO HIS FEET. All his annoying bounce and energy was back, and he was desperate to know every last detail.

'Did you get to speak to him? What did he say?'

I wanted to say, 'Nothing, because he's a hamster,' but I managed to hold it in.

'Where did he go? Did he look OK? Where do you think he might be?' The questions were tumbling out of him.

'I don't know where he is,' I said. 'But we need to find him before Mr Bugler does.'

'Yeah,' said Oscar. 'He hates having what he calls "unwelcome visitors" in the school. Do you remember the time he patrolled the playground with his broom for an entire afternoon because he thought he'd seen some pigeons in the area?'

'That's right,' agreed Amrita. 'He said he was worried they were going to ruin the playground with their beaks.'

'And he hates rodents even more than pigeons,' said Oscar.

Max started to look panic-stricken. Clearly, this wasn't helping. I tried to reassure him.

'Look, don't worry, Max,' I said. 'I'm sure we can find him, but the sooner we start looking, the better.'

We spread the word amongst our trusted friends, and we soon had a good-sized group of us out looking for Colin. And when lunch break rolled around, the same group of friends continued the search. One person was always on the lookout for Mr Bugler, while the rest of us scoured the playground and those parts of the school we were allowed into during break.

At one point, Max thought he saw Colin outside the kitchens. Something shot across the tarmac really quickly and disappeared under the bins, but when we searched the area, we couldn't find him anywhere. Another suspected sighting turned out to be a bit of fur off of someone's hood.

By the end of the lunch break, there was still no sign of Colin, and Max had become a bit tearful. I tried to reassure him that we could still find Colin, but now I had something else to worry about. The final of the baking competition was about to begin.

'Don't worry, Max,' said Amrita. 'We'll help you to look for him again during afternoon break. I'm sure he's going to turn up.'

And with that, I left my little brother in the capable hands of my two best friends and headed off to the cloakroom to get my stuff for the competition.

'Good luck, Cordie,' shouted Oscar, 'and save me a piece of that cake.'

'Thanks,' I shouted back in my weird high-pitched-when-I'm-nervous voice.

When I reached the kitchen, the other contestants were waiting outside the door while the kitchen staff finished clearing up after lunch. Having to wait in the corridor just made the situation even more tense and awkward. And, of course, Cleo Hawkins was her usual overconfident self. In fact, if there had been some officials there to measure it, I'm sure she could have broken the world record for smugness.

'I don't know about you guys,' she said, adjusting her insanely large bow, 'but I'm feeling pretty confident. I happen to know that Mr Pip's all-time favourite cake is Victoria sponge, and nobody bakes one quite like mine.'

Nobody said a word. We were either too nervous or too irritated to respond, so we all just looked at the floor.

There were five of us in the final. Me, Jake the Cake, the confused-looking boy from the previous round, and Cleo. There was also a Year 5 girl who I can honestly say I had NEVER seen at school before. In fact, I began to wonder whether she'd only joined the school in the last few days because she knew we were having a baking competition!

There was supposed to be another girl from Year 4 in the final, but she had phoned in sick that morning with a stomach bug. There was a rumour going around that she'd made herself ill from eating one of her own practice cakes!

As we continued the agonising wait outside the kitchen, I noticed how incredibly relaxed Jake the Cake looked. But then, with baking skills like his, he could afford to be relaxed. And even if he did run into any problems, he could just open his trusty notebook and look at all the ideas he'd written down during his billions of practice bakes.

There was no way I could compete with that kind of focus. My mind was all over the place. One minute, I'd be thinking about Colin the Hamster being chased by a broom-waving Mr Bugler. The next minute, an image of Cleo Hawkins's face covered in a custard pie would flash into my mind – which was how I was secretly hoping the competition would end!

Finally, the door to the kitchen opened, and we were ushered in to start the final.

'Find yourself a workspace and get all your ingredients out,' said Chef, 'and try to leave a bit of room between you and the other competitors.'

I found a spot, making sure I was nowhere near Cleo, and laid all my stuff out on the work surface. My heart was pounding. It was the moment of truth.

While we waited to start, I closed my eyes and imagined an alternative universe in which I would gently plant a big SLURPY custard pie right into Cleo's face. Ideally, the pie tin would then remain in place with the pie on her face, so that she looked like a big custardy robot. Aahh, lovely custard pie universe.

I was rudely awoken from my delightful daydream by the sound of Mr Pip's voice.

'You've got five minutes to organise yourselves and then we're going to begin the competition.'

'Oh, and don't touch the big potato masher,' added Chef, as he nervously stood in front of it.

I suddenly became aware of a commotion taking place to my left. When I looked across, I saw Jake the Cake FRANTICALLY looking through the bags he'd brought with him. All the calm he'd shown when we were waiting outside the kitchen had gone, and he now looked like a nervous wreck.

'What's the matter?' Mr Pip asked.

'It's my notebook,' Jake muttered, still desperately searching through his things. 'It has all my measurements and timings in it. We can't start until I've found it.'

'Well, I'm afraid you've only got a few more minutes to find it, Jake. I have to start the competition on time.'

The minutes ticked by, but after a lot of panic-stricken searching, an increasingly frantic Jake still hadn't found the notebook. Mr Pip cleared his throat and held up the stopwatch on his phone.

'The competition is about to begin!' he announced.

As I got ready to bake, I couldn't help wondering why Mr Pip was so eager to start on time. Was it really because he wanted to stick to the competition rules? Or was it just because he wanted to get his teeth into some cake as quickly as possible? Whatever the reason, the moment of truth had arrived, and I was about to find out whether I could actually bake, or whether I would soon be singing in front of the entire school.

Chapter 29

The competition began right on time, which meant that poor old Jake had to start baking without his trusty notebook. When I glanced over at him a few minutes into the final, all his legendary calm had completely evaporated, and he was crashing about the kitchen like a penguin on stilts. It was as if he had absolutely NO IDEA what he was supposed to be doing.

Cleo Hawkins, on the other hand, looked totally serene. She'd obviously baked her Victoria sponge cake plenty of times before and knew exactly what she was doing.

For the final, I'd decided to bake a chocolate fudge cake. I was really hoping it was going to give me an advantage when it came to the judging. My theory was that just like in 'Rock, Paper, Scissors', rock beats scissors every time – in my world, chocolate cake beats sponge cake every time. I just had to keep my fingers crossed that nobody made a paper cake!

I worked through my recipe as carefully as I could, and by the time I put the mix in the oven, I was quite hopeful it might turn out to be my best effort yet. I knew I was going to need a lot of luck to be able to compete with Cleo's Victoria sponge cake, but when I took my two halves of cake out of the oven, they actually looked pretty good. I still had to make the chocolate buttercream icing and put the halves together, but up to that point, things seemed to be going surprisingly well.

While the two halves of the cake cooled down, I carefully mixed up the icing, somehow resisting the temptation to test it. On any other day, I'd have happily eaten the whole lot with a BIG spoon, but I knew I had to control myself. As much as I LOVE chocolate, I LOVE not having to sing in front of the entire school even more. And I figured that a cake with no icing and teeth marks in it probably wasn't going to win.

I sandwiched the two halves together with a chocolate buttercream filling and then covered the outside of the cake with the remaining icing. I had to admit, it looked pretty scrummy and also quite professional. If I'd seen it in a café, I would definitely have wanted a slice. I just had to add a neat row of little fudge chunks around the edge for decoration, and I'd be finished.

'Five minutes,' shouted Chef. 'Your cakes should be almost ready now.'

I was busily adding the finishing touches, when I noticed some movement outside the window. It was afternoon break, and the playground was a hive of noise and activity. But that wasn't what had distracted me. What had caught my eye was my little brother Max chasing something small, beige and fluffy across the playground. He was closely followed by Oscar and Amrita and a very angry-looking Mr Bugler, who was waving a broom. I was so absorbed in watching the chase that I almost didn't hear Chef speaking.

'OK, everyone, time's up,' he said. 'Step away from your cakes and take a well-earned rest.'

I looked around at the cakes lined up on the work surface. They all looked pretty good and, I have to say, mine certainly didn't look out of place. All the effort I'd put in practising during the week seemed to have really paid off.

The one exception to all the great-looking cakes was Jake the Cake's effort. It was A COMPLETE MESS. I felt so sorry for him. He'd obviously planned to bake some sort of spectacular tiered cake, but what he ended up with was more like the Leaning Tower of Pisa covered in a layer of lumpy icing. And to make matters worse, it looked like it was going to topple over any minute.

But more worryingly, Cleo's Victoria sponge cake was spectacular. And the longer I stared at it, the more I became convinced that my only chance of winning would be if I ate her ENTIRE cake so it couldn't be judged.

As we carefully carried our cakes over to the judging table, Mr Pip couldn't take his eyes off the Victoria sponge. He wasn't even looking at any of the others. If Chef felt the same way, then it was probably going to take an actual real-life miracle for me to win.

'Well done, everyone,' said Chef, as he looked at the row of cakes. 'You've all done very well. Mr Pip and I will now sample each of them, and then we'll announce the winner.'

And with that, he took out a big kitchen knife and cut two slices of Cleo's Victoria sponge cake, then handed one of the plates to Mr Pip. When he took his first mouthful, Mr Pip looked like he had been transported to some kind of CAKEY WONDERLAND. At one point, his eyes even whirled around in his head and I thought he was going to float up off the ground like you see in cartoons.

'An excellent cake,' said Chef, after trying his slice. 'I can't think of a single criticism. Very well done.'

Mr Pip didn't say anything. He was still savouring the slice Chef had cut for him. Eventually, after he'd chased the last crumb around the plate, he spoke.

'That was SUPERB!'

At that point, I was convinced my fate was sealed, and the rest of the judging would be Chef and Mr Pip just going through the motions. And they were just about to move on to Jake the Cake's offering, when the door BURST open and to my shock Max bounded into the kitchen, closely followed by Oscar and Amrita, and a furious-looking Mr Bugler.

'What on earth is going on here?' barked Chef, as they charged around his kitchen. Panic-stricken, he dashed over to his giant potato masher and threw himself in front of it to protect it.

'It's Colin!' shouted Max. 'We saw him come in here.'

'There it is!' shouted Mr Bugler, spotting Colin cowering in the corner and rushing towards him, waving his broom.

He brought the broom down on the hamster as hard as he could, but at the last minute Colin dodged the blow, leapt onto Mr Pip's ankle and started scrambling up the outside of his trouser leg in a desperate bid to escape. Before Mr Pip had time to react, Colin had already reached the top and jumped onto the work surface. And from there, he headed at top speed straight towards... MY CAKE!

How could this be happening? One minute, I was admiring my lovely cake that just might help me beat Cleo. The next, I was facing the very real chance that it was going to have a hamster-shaped hole in the side of it, and I'd end up with a date in my diary for a karaoke performance I was NEVER going to live down!

As Colin headed towards my chocolate fudge cake – his little hamster legs scrabbling frantically along the shiny surface – I found it hard to watch. He was about to plough into the cake and destroy all my hard work. Either that or Chef and Mr Pip were going to have to judge it with a hamster embedded in the side of it. But just before reaching it, Colin jumped into the air, turned a somersault, and landed on the other side with a crash. The cake was SAVED. I was still in with a chance!

But Colin didn't stop there. The momentum carried him way beyond the cake and he was now seriously out of control, skidding along the slippery work surface at lightning speed. As he disappeared over the edge, it looked as though he was plummeting to a grizzly end.

'Colin!' shouted Max.

But Colin was in luck. By some miracle, he landed with a massive SPLAT on the chair that Cleo had rested her bag on. As he did, the sheer force of his landing knocked Cleo's bag off the chair, spilling the contents out onto the floor. And there was one item that immediately caught everyone's eye. It was JAKE THE CAKE'S NOTEBOOK. Cleo Hawkins had been hiding it inside her bag.

'That's my notebook!' Jake shouted. 'What's it doing in your bag?'

In the confusion that followed, nobody noticed Max grab hold of Colin – who was completely unharmed – and rush out through the doors. Before Mr Bugler even knew what was happening, Max and Colin were gone. The rest of us just stared at Cleo as she desperately tried to explain why the notebook was in her bag. She gabbled a few nonsensical words before realising it was pointless.

'I'm really sorry,' she said, staring at the floor. 'I don't know why I did it.'

'Well, whatever the reason was,' said Chef, 'I'm afraid you're disqualified from the competition.'

Mr Pip nodded solemnly in agreement. He then turned and stared at the Victoria sponge as if he was going to cry, clearly HEARTBROKEN at the possibility that it might be taken away from him forever.

At that point, nobody really knew how the competition could continue. Chef and Mr Pip went into a huddle in the corner and talked in really low voices for several minutes. But it was clear that they weren't getting any closer to deciding what to do. Although, at one point, I thought I heard Mr Pip suggest that he should take the Victoria sponge away as evidence.

And then Amrita, who was still hanging around with Oscar after the hamster hunt, said, 'What about calling it a draw?'

'Yeah, and we can all celebrate by having a slice of cake,' said Oscar.

'A draw?' said Chef. 'That's an interesting idea.'

'And so is the idea about having a slice of cake,' said Mr Pip.

'Yes,' I said. 'That's what we should do. After all, Jake never really had a chance, and it's unfair to judge him on what he's baked today. We should call it a four-way tie and declare that we've all won.'

The mystery girl from Year 5 was happy to agree, and the confused-looking boy nodded and even managed a confused-looking smile.

'Good,' said Mr Pip, 'we're all in agreement then. Congratulations, everyone, you're all winners.'

And then, without waiting to be asked, he immediately carved himself another massive slice of Cleo's Victoria sponge.

Mr Bugler was still in the kitchen, shining a torch under the ovens, with a look of fierce determination on his face. He hadn't been able to keep up with what had been going on, so he was unaware that Max and Colin had ducked out into the corridor some time ago.

'Sorry about the intrusion, Chef,' he said, 'but I noticed a mouse in the playground and I thought it might have come in this direction.'

I'd been so preoccupied by the whole CAKE AND HAMSTER thing that I'd forgotten all about the result. Now that Cleo had been disqualified, I guess I'd won the forfeit. I looked over at her. She was sitting on the floor, silently putting everything back into her bag.

'So, are we going to try your cake, then?' said Oscar, turning to me with a hopeful smile. 'It looks yummy.'

'Yes,' said Amrita, 'and even though there's been a rodent in the area, I think I might try some too.'

This was HIGHLY unusual for Amrita. The pressure of planning her party, combined with an afternoon of watching a rodent running around the school, had obviously tipped her over the edge. So, before she had a chance to change her mind, I cut three large slices of the cake and handed them around. I had to admit, it tasted FANTASTIC. And my victory over Cleo made it taste even better. In fact, it tasted so good we all had a second slice, and there was even some left for Mr Pip to try. It didn't mean much now the competition was over, but it still felt good to hear him grunt his approval.

And that's not all – Amrita liked it so much that she asked if I'd bake a cake for her birthday!

Chapter 30

As I gathered up my utensils and stuffed them back into their bags, the forlorn figure of Cleo appeared beside us. All her usual arrogance had disappeared, and she now had a look of dread on her face that people get when they're on their way to the dentist. Even her GIGANTIC bow had slipped from its usual position and now looked more like a deflated party balloon.

'So, I'll ask Mrs Collins if I can sing a solo in assembly next week then,' she said, finding it hard to look at me. She mumbled the words through gritted teeth, so I could tell she wasn't taking this well.

I know I should have felt triumphant. After all, I'd been waiting for the chance to put Cleo Hawkins in her place for years. But now that the moment had actually arrived, I didn't know whether I wanted to go through with it. I couldn't help thinking how humiliated I'd have felt if I'd had to get up and sing in front of everyone.

I knew what I had to do wasn't going to be easy, so I paused and took a deep breath first.

'I tell you what,' I said, still not quite believing what I was about to say next. 'I didn't get to try any of your Victoria sponge cake because Mr Pip got there before me, but it looked like it could have won the competition.'

'So what?' said Cleo, looking at the floor.

I took another deep breath. I was now so full of air I was worried I might do a giant burp when I tried to speak.

'If you bake a huge Victoria sponge tonight, so there's enough for the whole class to have some as their morning snack tomorrow, I'm prepared to forget the forfeit.'

Cleo looked at me as if I had just landed from another planet, and I knew that if our roles had been reversed, there was no way she'd let me off the hook so easily.

'But why?' she said. 'You won the bet. Why aren't you making me carry out the forfeit?'

'I'd just rather let the whole thing go,' I said, shrugging casually.

There were a few seconds of stunned silence while Cleo tried to come to terms with what I'd said.

'Erm. OK,' she said, still looking utterly confused. 'I'll bring the cake in tomorrow.'

Clearly worried that I might change my mind, she turned and walked quickly towards the kitchen door, still shaking her head in disbelief.

So, that was it. The competition was over, and the threat of public humiliation had finally been lifted. As I walked back to the cloakroom with Amrita and Oscar, I felt a massive sense of relief. But it wasn't long before I noticed that they were both looking at me weirdly.

'What was the real reason for letting Cleo off the hook?' asked Amrita, narrowing her eyes and staring at me intently.

'To be honest, I was just so grateful that I didn't have to do the singing thing, I thought I'd just let it go and move on.'

'And?' Amrita asked, clearly not satisfied with the answer I'd given.

'And Cleo's already in a lot of trouble over stealing Jake the Cake's notebook, so I thought that was kind of like a forfeit, anyway.'

'And?' she said, still not convinced.

'And... I REALLY didn't want to have to hear her sing. She makes my duck singing sound acceptable. In fact, compared to Cleo, I sound like an extremely talented duck.'

They nodded in agreement.

'Do you think this experience will help Cleo to change?' said Oscar, in his usual naïve and optimistic way.

'No,' I said. 'In fact, I wouldn't be surprised to find some old twigs in my slice of cake when I bite into it tomorrow. Anyway, if anyone's going to learn something from all this, I hope it's going to be ME. I will NEVER get involved in game of forfeit again.'

When I arrived home from school, Dad was outside loading Gran's bags into our car. The builders had phoned Mum during the day and it was good news – Gran's house was now safe and it was OK for her to move back in.

Gran couldn't wait to ask me how the competition had gone. When I explained that it had turned out to be a draw, everyone seemed a bit surprised: everyone except me and Max, of course. We just gave each other a knowing smile as if to say 'if only they knew the whole story'.

'And Colin turned up at school today!' said Max excitedly, holding up his little furry friend. 'I think he just fancied a day out.'

'Yes, and he had quite an adventure,' I said.

'Oh, how lovely,' said Gran. She leaned forward and stroked his little head. 'Nice to have you back, Colin.'

'We're going to miss having you here, Gran,' I said.

'I'm going to miss being here, too,' she said, smiling back at me. 'Although, I have to admit, I am looking forward to sleeping in my own bed again. It was very kind of you to give up your bedroom, Cordie, but there's nothing like sleeping in your own bed to help you get a good night's sleep. And I did miss having Mr Wallace sleeping in my room at night.'

I couldn't BELIEVE it. Gran actually MISSED having Mr Wallace with her in the night. I could only think that she must have completely lost all sense of smell in one of her frequent DIY accidents. Or maybe she just stuffed one of her beloved bananas up each nostril to block out the stench.

Whatever the reason, I had to agree with her about getting to sleep in your own bed. I couldn't wait!

So, all in all, it had been a great day. I'd beaten Cleo Hawkins and avoided having to sing solo in front of the entire school. AND that night I wouldn't have to sleep on the landing with Stinko the Wonder Dog sniffing and slurping away at my head. Oh, and Max had found Colin, so things were back to normal in Hamster World, too.

We gave Gran a hug and a kiss and watched as she climbed into the car beside Mr Wallace. But within a matter of seconds, Dad had opened the window and was hanging his head out, gasping for air. If only we could bottle that dog's farts, we could probably power the car on them. It would save the family a fortune on petrol!

As the car pulled away, I stood on the doorstep and waved, thanking my lucky stars that I had such a weird and wonderful gran. It's not everyone who can claim to have a superhero as a grandma. We watched as Pastry Woman rode off into the sunset. Another mission successfully completed.

'So did you see Colin's somersault today?' said Max. 'We've been practising that for weeks. It was awesome, wasn't it?'

My instinct was to argue with him, but for once I had to admit my little brother was right. After all, if Colin hadn't arrived when he did, I might have lost the competition.

'It was pretty spectacular, Max,' I said. 'And what about knocking the bag onto the floor at the end? Did you teach him that as well?'

'No, that was just something he improvised,' said Max. 'But let's face it, when you're dealing with a raw talent like Colin, anything's possible. Come on, Colin, let's go upstairs and practise those cartwheels I've been teaching you.'

It was such a relief to have my bedroom back again. I lay on my bed for the next half-hour and smiled as I relived the baking competition. I didn't even mind the sound of Max's hamster training coming through the walls. Maybe he was right. Maybe he would end up as a hamster handler after all.

So, that was my story. And what have I learned? Well, let's see.

>   1. Hamsters might, MIGHT, not be as stupid as they look.

>   2. NEVER bake a calculator into ANYTHING.

3. ALWAYS check your bag for rodents before leaving the house.

4. Fizzy, stringy cheese pie may actually CATCH ON.

5. Icing sugar is NOT a snack, and...

6. NEVER underestimate your gran!

Acknowledgements

Many thanks to Frances Moloney and Gareth Collinson for their meticulous edits; also to Vince Reid for his wonderful cover design and internal illustrations. Finally, I'm hugely grateful to my husband, Martin, for his tireless support and invaluable guidance.

Thank you for taking the time to read about Cordie and her friends. If you enjoyed the story, I'd be very grateful if you could leave a review on the book's Amazon page. Even one short sentence would be very much appreciated.

Many thanks

Annie Burchell

Printed in Great Britain
by Amazon